Educating the Will

by

Michael Howard

AWSNA

Printed with support from the Waldorf Curriculum Fund

Published by:

**The Association of Waldorf Schools
of North America
3911 Bannister Road
Fair Oaks, CA 95628**

Title: *Educating the Will*
Author: Michael Howard
Editor: David Mitchell
Proofreader: Ann Erwin
Photography: David Mitchell and Michael Howard
Cover: Hallie Wootan
© 2004 by AWSNA
ISBN # 1-888365-46-3

Table of Contents

FOREWORD

In February 2000 I was invited to give a keynote lecture at the Midwest Waldorf Teachers' Conference in Detroit, Michigan, on the theme of "Educating the Will." Although this theme has been central to my on-going work as a sculptor and sculpture teacher of both children and adults, the invitation to give a lecture was a call to clarify and deepen my understanding of will and its development.

The more I probed the nature of will the more I realized that I had embarked into mostly uncharted waters. I began to see that the prevailing understanding of will is rather simplistic and superficial. And only minimal attention seems to be given to the particular task of developing will in the children entrusted to us. As parents and teachers we cannot concern ourselves solely with the development of body and mind, leaving the will and feeling to chance. Human beings cannot be healthy unless they are whole. They cannot be whole unless the full spectrum of their human potential is fostered. For our children to be whole we must be able to help them develop their will and feeling with as much insight and intentionality as we bring already to the development of their intellect.

After giving my initial lecture I felt like I was more at the beginning of a task than at the end. So I have continued to work at elaborating and refining my thinking on the development of will by writing an essay. A grant from the Research Institute for Waldorf Education allowed me to devote time and energy over a two-year period to this enterprise. The Institute's Research Bulletin first published this essay entitled "Educating the Will" in three parts: Part I, January 2002, Part II, June 2002, and Part III, January 2003.

I am indebted to the Bulletin editors, Roberto Trostli and Douglas Sloan, for their steadfast encouragement and guidance in both the content and form of my writing. I cannot begin to name, but wish to acknowledge my gratitude to all the colleagues and students who over the years have contributed directly or indirectly to the evolution of my thinking and practical experience concerning the development of feeling and will. In particular, I want to thank my wife Susan for both her inner and outer support in all my ups and downs. More than anyone, she has indulged my thinking out loud and serves as my most reliable sounding board to what rings true. As my talking partner she often offered an essential missing thought, and I credit her as my ever-willing in-house editor with much of the improvements made from first to last draft. I am grateful to David Mitchell for his encouragement to transform my essay into a book. It was his inspiration and prodding that led me to add the fourth chapter in which I outline practical ideas for teaching the arts and crafts through the grades with the development of the will and feeling more consciously in mind. David was very generous in giving time from his busy schedule to take many of the photographs in the book which, in turn, got me started towards taking most of the remaining images.

As the practical work of completing this book comes to a close, the sense of being at the beginning of a great and vital enterprise only intensifies. As the work has evolved over the last four years, the dimension that has come most vividly into focus is the need to develop the will and feeling not only as distinct dimensions of our humanity but as a harmonious whole. The potential of our feeling nature to mediate and thereby harmonize our thinking and will led me in the course of writing to see the significance of developing what I call, "feeling-will." Although the title "Educating the Will" stands, it is the education of the feeling-will—the development of head, heart and hand co-ordination, as compared with merely head and hand co-ordination—that I see as the next frontier of education and culture. I perceive an urgent need for educators to become more actively engaged with the development of feeling-will.

Stated simply, if not boldly: we have given the last five hundred years to developing the scientist in each human being. We have much to be grateful for all we have gained through our scientific capacities. But if our eyes are clear-sighted, we will see evidence of unwanted side effects in all domains that can be attributed to the one-sided development of our abstract intellect and our disposition for mechanistic methods. Another side of our humanity lies largely under-valued and under-developed. In each human being there is an artist that is the healthy complement to the scientist. When developed, the artist in us has capacities that serve other essential aspects of human life and society. Like Icarus of the ancient world, we are at risk in our day of a mortal fall if we continue to soar to ever-greater heights drawing solely upon our existing powers without heeding the symptoms of our one-sidedness that tell us we have another side to develop.

To develop the feeling-will potential of each individual is to develop the artist in each human being. To develop the artist in each human being is the next great frontier in our evolution. The development of the artist in us, of our feeling-will, calls for the same dedication of our time and resources over the coming decades and centuries as we have given to the development of the scientist in us over the past centuries. As we do so, we can expect a different but equally radical enhancement in the quality of human life. We will discover new faculties and capacities that are as vital to social and economic life as to cultural life. In developing the eyes of the artist in us we will begin to see realities of the world and other people that otherwise elude us. It is in our blindness that we do most unintentional harm. When we can draw upon and harmonize the complementary nature of both the scientist and artist in us we will become more whole individuals capable of creating a more whole society.

— Michael Howard
Amherst, MA
January 2004

CHAPTER 1

Spirit-Will and Individuality

The education and teaching of the future will have to set particular value on the development of the will and feeling nature. Feeling and will are left more and more to what is called chance, because there is no insight into the real nature of will.

— Rudolf Steiner
The Foundations of Human Experience, Lecture 4

The Need for Insight into Will

If our intent as teachers and parents is to develop our children's full human potential, we will want to educate their feeling and will with as much insight and care as we bring to the development of their thinking. We will seek every means to deepen our insight into the nature and development of feeling and will.

The will is often equated with action, with moving our limbs. If educating the will is simply a matter of exercising our limbs, then physical exercise will suffice. Regular exercise is essential to healthy development, but developing our will is more than exercising our limbs. With our limbs we engage in outer activity. Behind the outer activity there is the inner activity of thoughts, feelings, desires, and motives. Will belongs to the inner activity behind the outer activity. Will is the inner force behind the outer force of our limbs.

Perceiving Will

We readily perceive outer actions, both our own and those of others. Can we perceive the inner activity of the will as clearly and as consciously as outer activity? To educate the will we must learn to perceive will.

When we learn a new capacity, such as riding a bicycle or driving a car, when we try to change a habit such as smoking, or transform impatience into patience, we are challenged to make an inner effort. The more difficult the challenge, the more we feel the intensity of this inner effort. When we observe this inner effort, we are no longer observing outer reality but an inner reality.

How this inner force translates into outer deeds remains largely unconscious. We have a thought, an intention; we move our hands and legs. But how a thought or feeling moves the muscles of our limbs is outside our waking consciousness. Science can describe some of the physiological and biochemical processes that go on in our body, but we are not conscious of these processes. We are well aware of the outer effort required to perform some physical work or athletic activity. Similarly, we can be conscious of our inner effort, which is typically greater when we are learning a new capacity. Wherever we perceive our inner effort we are observing our will.

As a teacher of sculpture, I have some students who approach clay modeling with great exuberance and self-assurance. Some of these energetic students produce beautiful, well-formed sculptures. Others, however, push and pull the clay with gusto and yet never arrive at a well-formed sculpture. In contrast, there are other students who are quite inhibited and who, not surprisingly, make sculptures that are tentative and weak. And yet, not infrequently, it is a student who lacks confidence who surprises everyone including himself, by producing an exceptional sculpture.

What do such observations reveal about the will of my students? How do these observations help me guide the students in developing their will? Are exuberance and energy expressions of a strong and healthy will? Are passivity and inhibition signs of a weak will? Does the capacity to create well-articulated forms reflect a strong will and a poor forming capacity a weak will?

To all this we must add the question of the student's inner effort. A student could work with great energy and produce a well-formed sculpture but have exercised little inner effort. Another equally energetic student might not produce as good a sculpture, but nonetheless gives her best effort. In such a situation the finished work of the two types of students does not necessarily reflect the quality of their inner effort and thus of their will.

And what are we to make of the inhibited student who produces formless sculptures? Surely, a lack of outer effort and mastery of basic skills is a clear indicator of a weak will. And yet it is possible that it is just the student who appears most blocked and produces weak work that could be developing a stronger will. Just because someone has more to overcome they must exercise more effort. That inner effort strengthens the will independent of outer results. The time frame and way that the will develops in each person touches the deepest mysteries of human individuality. For this reason, we must be cautious about judging inner effort and strength of will based on outer appearance and results alone.

We may think we are able to assess when others are exerting inner effort, and perhaps some of the time we can. But the more we realize how little we consciously perceive our own will, the more cautious and modest we might feel about our capacity to assess the strength or weakness of another individual's will. The recognition of our own limitations to perceive will can serve as a positive impetus for learning to perceive will directly and more vividly.

Willed Thinking

If as parents and teachers we want to better perceive and serve the developing will of our children we have no better starting place than to observe will more clearly in ourselves. We will not do this in the context of outer action, as we might expect, but in the activity of thinking. For example, we can choose a simple object such as a pencil, knife, or spoon and for a few minutes develop a train of thought that is exclusively related to that object. The person who can stay focused on the object for more than a few seconds without wandering off into unrelated thoughts and feelings is rare. In everyday life, we may think we are in control of our thoughts, but this seemingly simple exercise challenges any such assumption. The inner challenge of this thinking exercise reminds me of a group of kayakers I once observed paddling a rushing stream.

The kayakers were strong and expert paddlers. As they paddled downstream they displayed incredible mastery, going wherever and however they fancied. There seemed to be no limit to what they could do, including paddling directly upstream against the raging torrent. I was captivated as I watched some of them move slowly upstream—10, 20, 30 feet. Incredibly, some could paddle as much as 100 feet against the current, but sooner or later, even the strongest and most skillful paddlers would run out of steam. Instantly they would be swept back downstream by the relentless force of the current.

The skill of these kayakers can be compared to the skill of a good thinker who maneuvers confidently in the realm of thought. Just as there is downstream and upstream paddling, we can speak of downstream and upstream thinking. A novice thinker can be compared to a novice kayaker who splashes about ineffectively and consequently is soon over-powered by the force of the stream. A logical thinker, by comparison, exhibits great mastery in moving freely and effortlessly within the stream of thought. However, logical thinking is carried by logical necessity. In this sense, logical thinking is downstream thinking. A logical thinker can thus be compared to a kayaker who has mastered downstream paddling.

Only thinkers who cultivate the inner will to build thought upon thought without being swept along by random thoughts or automatic logic can be compared to a kayaker who is able to paddle upstream. The ability to develop even a simple train of thought without any compelling factors, if only for a few moments, is to think upstream. Otherwise, thinking streams through us from morning to night, largely beyond our awareness and control. When we try to build our own train of thought we discover that we are inwardly quite feeble relative to the strength of the stream of thought that otherwise flows through us. The so-called freedom of thought we exercise in daily life is actually the freedom of going with the stream of thinking. Thinking, as we commonly know it, is unfree thinking, because we are compelled to go with the stream that flits arbitrarily from one thought to another or is bound by logical necessity. To resist the compelling force of both of these forms of down-stream thinking requires inner strength of will. Free thinking is willed thinking.

By doing a simple exercise such as developing a train of thought about an object, we perceive the activity of will and see how it can be developed in us through the transformation of unfree thinking into ever more free thinking. The line between free and unfree thinking is not hard and fast. In fact, the process of developing will in thinking actually begins with logical thinking in the same way that downstream paddling is a step towards upstream paddling.

Thinking-Will

We can observe another dimension of will through a different exercise. In this case, we do a simple outer action that serves no practical need or purpose. For example, we move an object from one position to another. We do this not once but daily for an extended period of time, at least a month. Our will is engaged in carrying out this deed, but the will involved in activating our limbs is minimal. The real challenge of this exercise lies in finding the will to remember every day to do this simple act when there is no need or purpose compelling us to do it. Insofar as we are driven in our actions by a need or desire, we are unfree in our will. Conversely, only when we are not compelled by any outer or inner need can we claim to act with free will. Every time we fail to do this exercise, once we have committed ourselves to doing it, demonstrates that free will is neither an easy or common matter. We discover that our impulses to action are also a stream that flows through us. We feel free to paddle this way or that, but we are unaware that our choices are almost always with, rather than against, an unconscious and thus an unfree stream of will.

Freedom of choice is not the same as freedom of will. Insofar as will is an unconscious force sweeping us into action, we are inherently unfree. We become free in our will only when we take hold of our will impulses through our thinking, raising unconscious impulses to conscious motives. The will exercise described above challenges us to think the deed anew each day. We must develop the will to do it, but more importantly, we must develop the will to think it. Thinking the deed enables us to do it, and also to know why we do it. To know our motivation for action is to counter the unconscious and therefore unfree dimension of our will. Thinking must imbue will activity for it to be free will. Free will is thinking-will.

Free Will

We may go where we will, say what we will, and do what we will. Outwardly, we may appear, even to ourselves, to exercise free will. As long as no external agent obstructs our will, we are blessed with outer freedom. Outer freedom is a gift that can never be taken for granted. However, outer freedom is not inner freedom. When compelled from outside ourselves, we are physically unfree. Similarly, when compelled from within, we are inwardly or spiritually unfree. Outer freedom belongs to the dignity of every human being, but it is incomplete without the complementary development of inner freedom. If we are inwardly unfree when exercising outer freedom, our outer freedom is largely an illusion that works against our well being.

So much has been achieved in the last centuries regarding outer freedom. An equally great and arduous frontier lies before mankind to grasp the nature and significance of inner freedom. All the efforts and accomplishments to win outer freedom will bear fruit only to the degree that humankind employs education and other means for the development of inner freedom. The mysteries and challenges posed by human will are at the center of this new cultural frontier where we encounter the need to find practical answers to the questions: What is free will? When are we unfree in our will? How can we develop free will? To educate the will means to develop free will.

Observing the "I"

We have observed our own will as the inner effort to resist the compelling forces in our thinking. We have seen that freedom in our thinking depends on exercising will in thinking. In order to observe our will activity we had to exercise it. Thus, in observing our will we exercise our will. Likewise, we have observed another side of will as the unconscious and therefore compelling force behind our everyday actions. We have seen that inner freedom in our will calls for self-directed thinking.

If we are attentive in these thinking and willing exercises, we will make an additional observation. When trying to exercise willed-thinking we can observe our "I" initiating the inner effort of will to direct our thinking. Likewise, when trying to cultivate thinking in our willing we can observe our "I" thinking the thought that leads to our action. Cultivating inner freedom in both our thinking and willing provides opportunities to observe our "I" as the agent actively determining which thoughts and will impulses live in and through us. No matter how fleeting our success to master our thinking or our willing we can feel the very effort as a strengthening of our will. If only for a few seconds, we can feel this enhancement of will as an enhanced sense of "I." We feel our "I" is stronger. This experience begs the question: what is the relationship between a strong will and a strong "I"? In order to come to a full picture of the will, in particular free will, we must clarify what we mean by a strong "I," a strong individual. Toward this end we will also need to clarify the difference between a strong individual and a strong personality.

Typically a strong personality has a strong will, overflowing with energy to get things done. Such a strong personality is also a strong individuality if and when she is not driven or compelled to action, that is, when exercising free will. The signature of weak individuality, even in a strong-willed personality, is a lack of self-mastery, of unfree will. Similarly, someone who appears to have a weak will, and in that sense might be regarded as a weak personality, would actually prove to be a strong individuality when making the inner effort to overcome any inherent weakness such as a lack of energy and initiative.

The capacity described above, to win a degree of freedom in our will through thinking, enables us to tame an over-active will or to stimulate an under-active will. Whether we have a strong or weak personality, a strong or weak bodily constitution is, in the first instance, something outside our control. However, it is our individuality, our "I," that can decide how to meet our outer and inner limitations. "I" choose to resign myself passively to my given constitution and personality or to become inwardly active in transforming my original limitations. All efforts to transform and balance our given bodily and soul constitution, however modest and slow, are deeds of our "I," our individuality. In fact, such inner striving is a prime way that our individuality develops.

If our intention as parents and teachers is to develop the whole human being, the whole child, then we must provide every opportunity for children to develop their thinking, feeling and will natures. Equally, we must attend to the nurturing of their "I" as that which takes hold of their bodily and soul constitutions. We must guide children to unfold their full potentials, not only of their body and soul, but also of their spirit individuality. Every child is a unique individual. Every parent, teacher and public official understands and supports the need for education to serve the development of each individual, to unfold the unique gifts and potential of each child. But can we say we truly perceive each child's budding individuality? If talk about the individual is to be more than rhetoric or good intentions, then we must be more rigorous in our efforts to understand the nature of individuality and the ways it is developed. This book attempts to clarify the nature and development of will as one avenue to better understanding the nature and development of individuality.

Different Forms of Will

From the above discussion, at least three different forms of will can be recognized. We have indicated that a strong or weak individuality or "I" is quite distinct from a strong or weak personality, which is different again from a strong or weak bodily constitution. In the descriptions of my sculpture students we saw that some are blessed with an abundance of energy while others have less. This energy belongs to will in the realm of the physical/etheric constitution. We will refer to it as "life-will."

The degree to which someone creates well-formed sculptures depends on an ability to integrate thinking, feeling and willing. A student may be able to picture a form but be unable to master the movements of her hands to make the form visible in the clay. Another student may be quite capable with his hands but may have difficulty visualizing the form in his mind's eye. In both cases we are looking at will within the soul or astral body. We will speak of will of this kind as "soul-will."

Lastly, the degree of effort a person makes, particularly in overcoming the limitations of his bodily and soul constitutions, originates from the will of the "I" or "spirit-will." If we are to educate the will, we must be clear about which form of will we are educating. In fact, we must clarify how these different forms of will are intrinsically related to each other.

I	—	individuality	—	spirit-will
Astral body	—	personality	—	soul-will
Etheric/physical	—	physicality	—	life-will

At first, such distinctions seem to make our understanding of will more confusing by making it more complicated. Equal to the danger of making a simple thing unnecessarily complicated is the risk of making a complex reality too simple. The latter is the case with our common understanding of will. Much confusion and misunderstanding about the will originates from the fact that we use the word "will" to cover a broad spectrum of reality. Imagine if we had only the word "color" and no names for the individual colors such as red, yellow and blue. The Eskimos have many different words for snow because their survival depends on their ability to be clear about the subtle but significant variations in snow. Similarly, our welfare may depend on our ability to distinguish subtle but significant differences in the forms of will.

We have differentiated three kinds of will that correspond to the three-fold human being of body, soul and spirit. In Lecture 4 of *The Foundations of Human Experience*, Rudolf Steiner elaborated no fewer than seven different forms of will that correspond with the seven-fold human being:

Physical body	—	instinct
Etheric body	—	impulse/drive
Astral body	—	desire
Ego	—	motive
Spirit self	—	wish
Life spirit	—	intention
Spirit man	—	resolve

In Chapter 3 we will see the significance of all seven forms of will, in particular the three higher forms. For now we will continue to develop our understanding of life-will, soul-will and spirit-will. The reader will note that for the sake of simplicity we have combined the physical and etheric thereby simplifying four forms of will to three. In itself, such a list of terms is abstract, making it difficult for us to find an inner connection and sense of relevance.

To counter this one-sidedness we will try to make the distinctions about will more concrete through an example. Picture a charioteer riding his chariot with the reins to his horses firmly in hand. We will compare the will of the horses to the will of the charioteer. The charioteer could reach his destination without using his horses—he could walk or he could pull his chariot himself. In this case the charioteer would exert the strength of his own limbs, he would exercise his own life-will instead of using the life-will of his horses. Perhaps the charioteer lacks the necessary strength or perhaps he simply wants to arrive at his destination more quickly and without exhausting his own life-will.

The charioteer's "wanting" or desire to go to a particular place in a particular manner is an expression of his soul-will, the will of his astral body. The horses may also have a will of their own. The horses may have lots of vitality, a strong life-will, but may display a stubborn will to go nowhere or a wild will to go everywhere except where the charioteer intends. This "will-of-their-own" exhibited by the horses is not their life-will, but their soul-will. A stubborn or wild horse has a strong soul-will of its own that may be in complete opposition to the equally strong but different soul-will of the charioteer. In a contest between soul-wills, the charioteer has no particular advantage over the horses. The charioteer has an advantage only in his potential to master the soul and life-will of the horses through his spirit-will. The potential advantage of the charioteer lies not simply in his power of thought which the horses also possess—both the charioteer and the horses have astral bodies—but in his potential to observe, learn from and

Fig. 1. The Charioteer of Delphi

alter his thinking through the activity of his spirit-will or "I."

   The spirit-will of our "I" is the charioteer. Thinking, feeling and willing are the three steeds of our soul that our "I" must master. Some of us have horses with a wild will, others have a stubborn will, and yet others have some combination of wild and stubborn, swinging back and forth without warning. Whatever kind of horses the charioteer gets, his task is to master their soul-will and life-will. Whether we have an excess or deficit of life-will, whatever strengths and weaknesses we have in our soul-will, the challenge of our spirit-will is the same—to master the life-will and soul-will that destiny has given us.

In summary, we can say that the charioteer exerts his life-will when he makes a physical effort. He exerts his soul-will when he makes an inner effort in thinking, feeling and willing, such as when directing his outer actions through thinking and feeling. Most importantly, the charioteer, unlike the horse, can learn from past experience and change the way he thinks and does things through self-initiated activity. The charioteer exercises his spirit-will only when his inner effort is directed towards developing new capacities and/or balancing one-sided tendencies in his bodily or soul constitution.

Soul-will and spirit-will both involve inner effort compared with the outer effort of life-will. For this reason soul-will and spirit-will are often confused. The primary characteristic of spirit-will is that the inner effort is self-initiated. For example, soul-will is exercised in learning to play a musical instrument. Spirit-will is engaged only when the individual makes that effort out of himself and not because a parent or teacher is making him do it. For this reason human freedom exists only when we exercise our spirit-will. In our life-will and soul-will we make choices and we make effort, but those choices and effort are done in freedom only when they are initiated by our spirit-will, our true individuality.

The thought that every outer and inner challenge is an opportunity to develop our spirit-will, our spirit individuality, by transforming the unfree elements of our life- and soul-wills gives meaning and purpose to life. Our life-will and soul-will may be strong or weak, however the spirit-will of our individuality is never too strong—in every case our individuality, as distinct from our personality, can be strengthened. The unfree elements of our bodily and soul natures serve a higher good; they provide the substance upon which our spirit individuality works. In cultivating spirit-will we develop our true individuality.

CHAPTER 2

Sense-Nerve Will and Feeling-Will

In Chapter 1 we came to see a relationship between inner effort, spirit-will and the development of human individuality. Taken together these thoughts shed a new light on the role of education and, for that matter, the deeper significance of all forms of culture. If the many facets of education and culture are the spokes of a great wheel, at the hub we find the spiritual striving of each human being to realize his or her true and full individuality.

It is well established that education must serve the development of each child's physical and mental potentials. We touched on this familiar aspect of education in discussing the development of life-will and soul-will. We introduced these terms in order to introduce the concept of spirit-will as distinct from soul-will and life-will. From the perspective developed here spirit-will is synonymous with the "I," the ego and individuality.

Such terms are needed, not as alternative jargon to be used or dismissed as suits our fancy but rather to expand our perception of human nature and thus the scope of education. If as parents and teachers we are committed to developing our children's full potential, then we cannot shy away from concerning ourselves with their deeper, most essential being, their spirit individuality. A child's individuality, that which says "I," must be distinguished from mind and body. Education develops mind and body, but more significantly, it develops spirit individuality through the inner effort that the individuality makes in taking hold of and mastering mind and body. The charioteer is spirit-will holding the reins of life- and soul-wills, the charioteer is the "I" that masters head, heart and hand.

From the above it is clear that we must provide opportunities for our children to master not only their thinking, but also their feeling and willing. Where their thinking, feeling or willing is underdeveloped or weak, we will help them to strengthen these capacities. However, we may also guide our children towards taming tendencies that are too strong. Educational goals must include the mastering of the too strong as much as the too weak aspects of their bodily and soul natures. In taking hold of both the too strong and the too weak in their nature our children develop their true individuality.

We will now consider more concretely how spirit-will is developed through the content and methods of educational activities. We saw in Chapter 1 that we develop our spirit-will by transforming the inherent limitations and thus unfree dimensions of our thinking and willing. We saw that this is achieved through the complementary efforts of bringing will into thinking and thinking into will. These inner activities were introduced through two simple exercises that in practice are not so easy. Simple or difficult, such thinking and will exercises are not usually incorporated into the curriculum for school children. And yet, every discipline we teach children can be seen as developing will-in-thinking or thinking-in-will.

Developing Will-in-Thinking

All schools teach the three Rs of reading, writing and arithmetic. Why do we teach our children to read and spell, to count, measure, add and subtract? Obviously, because they will need these capacities to function in today's world. But there is a deeper significance. In learning to master cognitive capacities such as reading, writing and arithmetic we exercise will-in-thinking and thereby develop freedom in thinking. *All cognitive activities develop will-in-thinking.*

Strictly speaking, no one needs to learn to think. From the moment we awake to falling asleep stream-of-consciousness thinking flows through us with the same necessity as the circulation of our blood. We take for granted that we wake up within an inner world of thoughts as much as we wake up in an outer world of objects. When we speak of learning to think we are referring to the process of ordering and elaborating the given world of thoughts which initially is limited and unformed. To a large extent this takes place through imitation of adult speakers and thinkers and thus without formal intervention. Formal education offers a broader scope of disciplines than would be expected within the informal circumstances of individual families. Thus, the implicit if not explicit intention of all formal education is to educate the whole human being, or at least more of human nature than individual circumstances might otherwise offer.

Whatever our educational perspectives, no one questions the importance of developing cognitive skills. There is less clarity and unanimity, however, when it comes to assessing the value of the arts and crafts. Not so long ago, the ability to knit and carve wood had practical value. Today such skills are no longer essential to the demands of life. However, if we concern ourselves with the inner capacities, and not merely the outer skills developed through art and craft activities, we discover their contemporary significance.

In these activities we exercise our limbs. As with thinking, no one needs to learn to move his limbs. However, our limbs would flail about as mere scribbling or wild running and crashing about if the movements of our hands and feet were not ordered and directed through the intentionality of thinking. Through the arts and crafts we learn to master our will through the power of thinking. *All art and craft activities develop thinking-in-will.*

Developing Thinking-in-Will

We will now look at specific activities in relation to developing not just the will but thinking-in-will. In this chapter I will not elaborate further on the specific ways that cognitive activities develop will-in-thinking. Although there is much to clarify about developing will-in-thinking through cognitive activities, I leave this task for others who are more experienced in this area. Not only is the development of thinking-in-will through the arts and crafts the area in which I have experience, but of the two, it is the one less understood and fostered through education today.

Lined vs. Unlined Paper

We will begin with a seemingly minor issue: to give our children lined or unlined paper on which to write. In most schools today it is common practice to give children lined paper without even considering the alternative of unlined paper. As adults we are so accustomed to using lined paper that the option of using unlined paper may simply never occur to us. Furthermore, if our intention is to get the best results, then lined paper will certainly increase the likelihood of uniform and legible writing. However, in giving children lined paper a developmental opportunity is missed. In writing without lines, *we must visualize and feel the straightness, we must feel and create the parallel lines.* In itself the capacity to write straight and parallel lines may not seem so important. Writing on unlined paper gains significance only when the exercising of thinking-in-will is an integral part of our educational goals. The significance of this becomes only clearer if we ask ourselves: why do we teach our children to write their letters? Why not from first grade let them use stencils, typewriters and word processors for writing?

Beyond the possibility that a mechanical writing device may not always be available, there is another good reason for children to learn to form their own letters. In punching keys (as I am at this moment) I am exercising will directed by thinking, but it is mechanical will. My will conforms to the mechanical demands of the machine. My will and the will of all other users of such a machine conform to the same mechanical activity. (I am not referring to the thinking activity that provides the *content* of what I write but to the thinking required by the *form* of writing.) It is not "I" thinking in my will, but my thinking-will conforming to the thinking-will embodied within the machine. By contrast, when I write by hand, I form the letters, I think in my will.

Writing on unlined paper is only an extension of forming our own letters. To abandon the use of unlined paper is a small, but not insignificant, step towards abandoning handwriting itself. As education becomes evermore driven by job readiness for the real world—ironically a world increasingly shaped by a virtual reality—it is not inconceivable that handwriting could follow the horse-drawn carriage into quaint obscurity. Whatever value handwriting may be losing from the practical side, it gains value when seen as a means for developing individuality through "I"-directed thinking-in-will.

Developing Feeling-in-Will

Handwriting on unlined paper has a further dimension of significance for human development. In describing the merits of writing without lined paper I used the words: " we must visualize and *feel* the straightness as we write, we must *feel* and create the parallel lines." The use of the word *feel* has particular meaning. Thusfar we have only discussed thinking-in-willing and willing-in-thinking. What about feeling? How is feeling developed in its own right? How does it develop in relationship to thinking and willing? We have seen how manual activities such as writing exercise thinking-in-will. We shall now consider the development of "feeling-in-will." I will try to characterize and demonstrate its development through the practical activity of carving a spoon in wood.

Two Ways to Carve a Spoon

There are many ways to make a spoon. I will describe two contrasting ways. Most people find woodwork intimidating because it is self-evident that once you take away wood you cannot put it back. For this reason, it is natural to assume that the shape of a spoon must first be drawn onto the wood and then cut out with a saw. Once the shape is cut out, gouges, rasps and sandpaper can be applied to refine and finish the final form of the spoon.

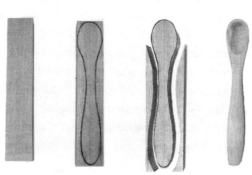

Fig. 2. The draw and cut way to make a spoon

If we are making wooden spoons for our livelihood, where speed of production has financial implications, the above method makes perfect sense. However, if our purpose is educational, other factors must be given weight. In particular we must ask ourselves: what capacities do we intend our students to develop? To draw and cut out the form of a spoon exercises head-and-hand coordination. It develops thinking-in-will or what I shall also refer to as "sense-nerve will." If, however, our intent is to develop head, heart and hand, or, thinking, feeling and willing, then we will look for other methods that allow feeling to be more active in itself and also as a mediator between thinking and the will activity of our limbs.

Strictly speaking we should speak of "thinking-feeling-will." However, the term, "feeling-will" flows better and it emphasizes that feeling can provide intentionality for our willing in the same way that thinking can. In fact the discussion that follows hinges on the distinction between actions based on thinking-in-willing as compared with feeling-in-willing. However, as used here feeling-will should be understood to include the thinking element and thus refers to the harmonious integration of thinking, feeling and willing. In contrast to thinking-in-will or sense-nerve will where only head and hands are engaged, feeling-will engages and harmonizes head, heart and hand.

Ultimately, our educational task is to develop the "whole" human being, the "whole child." However, it is simplistic to believe that we are educating the whole child simply by exercising head, heart and hand through cognitive, artistic and physical activities. To have art and crafts in any form is, in one sense, better than having none at all. On the other hand, there are different ways to work in the arts and crafts that develop not only different outer skills but, more significantly, quite different inner capacities. We can make a spoon, for example, in a sense-nerve manner or in a feeling-will manner. The first method of making a spoon described above represents a sense-nerve approach where the emphasis is given to analytical thinking and a mechanical process. How might we carve a spoon in a way that exercises the feeling-will?

We can cut a piece of wood so that it has a certain thickness, width and length. The proportion we give to the wood becomes part of the spoon's ultimate form. In a subtle but significant way it contributes to the feel of the spoon, for example, whether it will feel stout or delicate. We can decide the quality of proportion without having the final form of the spoon in our mind's eye. If our intent is to exercise the feeling-will then having a preconceived image of the form is not only unnecessary, it is to be discouraged. For this reason we will not draw any form on the wood. Instead, we can begin by asking ourselves: what aspects of the original block do we want to keep, such as its proportion, and what aspects do we wish to change? For example, if the wood is flat and angular, our hands will feel uncomfortable holding it, so we round off the corners. See Fig. 3, which illustrates the beginning of a feeling-will approach to making a spoon. Having eliminated the sharp corners, we realize that it still feels too large in diameter. So we rasp down the diameter, checking it by eye, but more importantly, testing it in our hands to see how it feels. We can do the same with the bowl of the spoon. We can make a shallow hollow to begin with, gradually enlarging and deepening it according to what our feeling and thinking suggest is appropriate for the eventual use of the

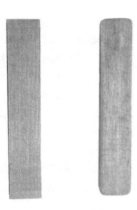

Fig. 3.

spoon. In this way the whole process from beginning to end is one in which we intuitively feel our way along. This is especially important when trying to find a harmonious connection between the handle and the bowl of the spoon.

Fig. 4. Only feeling-will can harmonize the form of a spoon from all sides.

Such an approach does not necessarily produce better results since all manner of beautiful spoons and other objects can be produced in the more mechanical, or sense-nerve manner. As educators what matters is that we guide an activity such as carving a spoon not merely according to our preference or habit but out of developmental criteria: do these children need to develop their sense-nerve will or their feeling-will?

It is quite conceivable that a woodcarving teacher would use the draw and cut process with one group or one student when it was felt that the sense-nerve side needed strengthening. In general, however, contemporary life and education already provide ample opportunities for children to develop the head and hand coordination of their sense-nerve will. The tools and methods of carving wood, in contrast to cutting wood, are particularly suited to exercising the more intuitive, feeling-will. In fact, to exercise feeling-will is the best, if not only, reason for including woodcarving in the curriculum of contemporary schools. If the development of the feeling-will is not among our pedagogical goals and the arts and crafts like woodcarving are not approached in ways that serve such development, then the view that the arts and crafts have little contemporary relevance will surely prevail.

To create something with one's own hands, if only once in one's life, is surely a healthy antidote against becoming passive consumers. However, the more primary reason for including woodcarving and the other arts and crafts in education, not as electives but as core activities, is to develop the feeling-will that in most people is under-developed. The feeling-will should be developed for its own sake, simply as an aspect of our human potential. However, there are other reasons, social reasons, why education must develop the feeling-will side of human nature.

Developing the Creative-Will of Social Sculptors

Forming a spoon or bowl through the activity of our feeling-will has significance far beyond the making of beautiful hand made objects. Every human being is a social sculptor who shapes and is shaped by social forms—political, economic, educational and cultural. For the most part social forms are created and implemented through abstract, analytical thinking; that is, they are implemented and executed through the activity of sense-nerve will. Contemporary life is ruled by the sense-nerve will. The sense-nerve human being is the side we educate and that most forms of work require. In today's world it is essential to develop the thinking-will of the sense-nerve human being. But we have established that the goal of education, as with human development in general, is to tame the too strong as much as strengthen the too weak. Today the sense-nerve will is over-developed and over-used as if it were the only way to be and act in the world. In fact there are other sides of our humanity such as the feeling-will that are under-developed and under-utilized. The sense-nerve will is the source of our greatest accomplishments, but it is also the root of our undoing when its limitations and one-sidedness are not balanced and complemented by the feeling-will. A healthy social life will depend more and more on human beings developing their feeling-will as the necessary complement to their sense-nerve will.

Because the feeling-will is underdeveloped compared to the overdeveloped sense-nerve will, we must seek every opportunity to develop the feeling-will. The capacity to feel the clumsiness of our spoon and to intuitively feel step by step how to make it harmonious has significance beyond spoon making. As it awakens and develops through activities such as woodcarving and other arts and crafts, our feeling-will can begin to manifest in other domains. For example, we will feel more intensely the rigidity and clumsiness of social forms. Such feeling perceptions will awaken our creative will to transform dead and chaotic social forms into more living and harmonious ones. In this way we will all become, what Joseph Beuys called, "social sculptors." In Chapter 3 we will explore more fully the social implications of developing feeling-will. Before doing so, we will look at a few other ways the feeling-will can develop through the arts and crafts.

Beeswax and Clay

The aspiration to educate the whole human being calls for careful reconsideration of many assumptions and habits. Details that in the past may have seemed minor now take on greater significance. For example, teachers who have the children model are to be commended whatever the material and method they employ. However, since most teachers are not sculptors, they are understandably grateful for any indications that give them direction. In Waldorf schools there is a prevailing view that from pre-school up through grade 3 children should model with beeswax. Promoting the merits of beeswax typically includes the judgment that clay should not be used with young children because it is harmful to them. The explanation commonly given is that the cold, wet clay robs the children's forces.

If this is the case, we may well ask if it is harmful for young children to play in puddles, streams, wet sand, mud, snow and the cold water from the sink? Playing with such materials can be messy and thus can cause some inconvenience, but I have never heard anyone say they are harmful. Quite the opposite, it is generally regarded as normal and healthy. If there is any reason for concern it surely is in regard to those children who avoid playing with materials such as sand and snow. One finds the same healthy delight and creative play in a group of children mucking out in a natural clay pit as in a sandbox.

Such observations alone are reason enough to be wary of the view that clay is inappropriate or harmful in the early years. Those who do not trust their own experience about the healthy nature of clay modeling may look to Rudolf Steiner for the definitive insight. Research by colleagues both in Europe and America has thus far found not one statement from Steiner that hints at harmful effects of clay at any age. On the contrary, Steiner said, "We continue this [fundamental artistic work in grades 1-4] by moving on to three-dimensional plastic forms, using plasticene if it is available and whatever else you can get if it isn't—even if it's the mud from the street, it doesn't matter. The point is to develop the ability to see and sense forms." Second Curriculum Lecture in *Discussions with Teachers*, p. 198.

I raise the issue of clay modeling for two reasons. As a sculpture teacher I feel called to challenge what seems an unfounded dogmatism in my realm of activity. But the use of clay is not the real issue. More significantly, it serves as an example where vigilance is called for. If we recognize a dogmatic mindset creeping into one or two areas of our educational work, however minor in itself, is it not likely that there are others? The issue I raise is the threat posed by a dogmatic mindset per se, where in the name of "best practice" any principle or method is fixed into the one-right-way. The reason we should be alert to even minor expressions of a dogmatic stance is because as a soul gesture it is the polar opposite of what makes education an art. To judge clay as harmful is to short-circuit a possibly creative pedagogical activity. Instead of judging clay as good or bad, we might ask ourselves: what does each material—beeswax, clay, sand, mud, wood, wool—offer for the development of different capacities? If our inner gesture is experientially open rather than conceptually closed, we open ourselves to appreciate the potential of one material to engage one aspect of human nature while another material may best be used to exercise another capacity.

We might discover that certain materials are best suited for sense-nerve activity while other materials lend themselves better to feeling-will activity. If we determine that we need to exercise their sense-nerve will, or what is commonly called head/hand coordination, then beeswax is well suited. The inclination to make recognizable objects—bowls, birds, and so forth, but especially, the fine fingertip manner of forming small shapes in wax engage the sense-nerve will. If on the other hand we wish the children to exercise their feeling-will, clay is particularly suitable. Clay can naturally be used in larger quantities that invite whole hand movements. This in turn allows the students to focus more on feeling the quality of the forms rather than on conceptual associations.

Often the beeswax that is used for modeling is brightly colored. Children and teachers alike may find these colors cheerful and fun, for example, a gnome with a red shirt, blue pants, and a green hat with a yellow feather. What are the pedagogical issues a teacher might consider regarding the color of beeswax? If we want the children to have a *color* experience, we have them paint. When painting they do not sculpt, they do not give three-dimensional form to the pigment. If we want them to have a form experience, we should help them focus on forming the clay or beeswax. In giving them colored beeswax we are distracting them from a full *form* experience; we are asking them to paint while they are sculpting. Put another way, using brightly colored beeswax stimulates the sense-nerve will. If our pedagogical intent is to develop the feeling-will through sculptural forming, then we would use clay or beeswax that has a simple earth tone.

Sense-Nerve or Feeling-Will Rhythm of the Day

In today's world to offer art and craft activities in any shape or form is better than to offer none at all. However, if our intent is to develop the feeling-will then it is not enough to simply have art and craft activities scheduled. At least two factors must be taken into consideration. The first requirement is that the art and craft activities are done in a manner that actually engages the feeling-will. In fact the way art and craft activities are approached today mostly exercises the sense-nerve will. Educators are largely in uncharted waters when it comes to finding the materials and methods that engage the feeling-will. Developing the feeling-will does not happen by itself; it must be nurtured through clear and persevering intent.

The second factor pertains to the context of the art and craft sessions within the daily rhythm of the school schedule. The art and craft activities themselves may be approached in ways that engage the feeling-will of the children, but the rhythm of the daily schedule of most schools is overwhelmingly sense-nerve. The sense-nerve character of the school day works against whatever nurturing of the feeling-will is taking place through the art and craft activities.

Waldorf schools have a long main lesson block, but the rest of the schedule is like most other schools with forty-five minute periods. The factors that determine a daily schedule of several short periods are: 1) most cognitive and performing art subjects work well within such a time frame; 2) this seems to be the only way to schedule all the required subjects. What is not given much, if any, consideration is that this typical daily rhythm originates from and supports the sense-nerve human being and not the feeling-will. When developing the sense-nerve human being is our legitimate goal, as in cognitive courses, a staccato, sanguine tempo of classes is appropriate. However, where our intent is to develop the feeling-will, the conventional rhythm of classes is inadequate, if not, counter-productive.

As long as both teacher and students remain conscious of time, as long as they cannot stop thinking and chattering about all-manner of other things, they have not found their way from their sense-nerve nature into their feeling-will. The feeling-will manifests as a focused and timeless absorption in the work at hand. Students who complain about how long a period is lasting do so because they are stuck in their sense-nerve nature. By comparison, the students who complain about how quickly the time has flown by feel rudely awakened from the legitimate dream-like world of their feeling-will as they are thrust back into the sense-nerve world.

As citizens of our time, most Waldorf educators and Waldorf students are by nature more at home in their sense-nerve nature. Humankind is becoming pathologically sense-nerve. Pathological is not too strong a term if we understand it to mean "compulsively" sense-nerve. In fact the greater danger is to underestimate the sense-nerve effects of our growing technological culture. Our children must be able to function in this sense-nerve world, but to live and work out of their full humanity they must develop their feeling-will as well.

Our intention may be to educate the whole human being but our educational practice has a long way to go. To be true to the ideal of educating the whole child we must distinguish our ideals from our deeds. We must recognize that our own education and the pressures of society are pressing us to over-emphasize the sense-nerve intellect and sense-nerve will. When it comes to educating the feeling-will we have hardly begun.

If we are truly dedicated to educate the whole human being, not just the sense-nerve, but equally the feeling-will, then we must attend to the overall character of the school's form as much as its content. At the end of his life Rudolf Steiner indicated in private conversation that he saw the need "to turn the rudder of Waldorf education 180 degrees." It is generally understood that he meant that arts and crafts were to become even more central. Given the reputation and self-image of Waldorf schools as already strongly committed to the arts, we may wonder what Steiner could have imagined. Is it not possible that he felt profound concern for the one-sided development of the sense-nerve human being compared with the relatively weak and undeveloped feeling-will human being? Did he feel the Waldorf school as he had formed it needed to do more in developing the feeling-will?

Rudolf Steiner was radical enough to suggest that a class teacher stay with his or her children through the eight years of the lower school. Might he have favored a rhythm of only three long periods each day, adding to the existing main lesson period a comparable late morning period for languages and performing arts and a whole afternoon for arts and crafts? The sense-nerve human being in teachers and students can find all-manner of reasons why the present schedule cannot and should not be changed beyond a little concession here and there. But if we only dared to try it, the feeling-will in us would blossom. We might then begin to discover the full reality of the whole human being. We might also discover what it means to develop the whole teacher and the whole school.

The Whole Teacher in a Whole School

If we aspire to educate the whole child, the whole human being, then we must concern ourselves equally with the development of the whole teacher and the whole school. When we speak about the whole child we mean body, soul and spirit. We mean head, heart, and hand, or the thinking, feeling and willing of each individual. How do these criteria of wholeness apply to the development of the whole teacher and the whole school?

To become whole human beings our children must not only engage in a full spectrum of activities which engage all of their potential faculties, they must also meet living models of human wholeness in real people. They need to meet the whole teacher in a whole school. Some may think this is an ideal beyond our reach. Rather than make excuses for ourselves, or burn out trying to do the impossible, there is a middle ground for us to explore.

Our children do not need teachers who are whole, they need models of striving towards wholeness. They do not need a school that is whole, it is quite enough that they experience a school community striving to become more whole. Furthermore, our children need not encounter the whole teacher in each individual teacher but in the community of teachers. In this sense, the whole teacher is synonymous with the whole school. Each individual teacher is inevitably one-sided, but with sufficient attention and care, the faculty can be guided by the ideal of wholeness as they form and re-form the constellation of human qualities and capacities among the faculty. This is already the case, insofar as a school community has a spectrum of different outer and inner capacities among its faculty. But there is more we can do.

If we recognize the need to give greater emphasis to the development of feeling-will in our schools, one significant step would be to create a place in the school community for individuals who actively cultivate the feeling-will in their discipline. For example, for a school to invite even one artist or craftsperson to join the school community, not as a teacher, but as an artist-in-residence with a working studio on campus, would have a far-reaching effect. To have an artist/craftsperson active in a working studio would give the children an experience of their feeling-will that the same artist/craftsperson in a teaching studio could not give to the same degree. To visit an artist's studio on an occasional class trip may be special but it implies, unspoken, that creative will activity is a novelty rather than a way of being. Even when not working with the students directly, an artist/craftsperson working in his or her studio would contribute a vital element to a school community that is committed to serving the development of the whole human being. If only to better serve our children we have reason to make our schools more than classrooms for sense-nerve teaching. They must become cultural centers where a rich diversity of cultural life serves adult development as an essential part of serving the development of the children. Instead of artists having to adapt the feeling-will nature of their work to the demands of a sense-nerve organization, schools must transform their organizational form to accommodate the feeling-will on its own terms.

Of course this can only happen if teachers and parents see the full meaning and implications of educating the whole human being. But here we touch a sensitive point. To the extent that we ourselves are at home in the full spectrum of our human nature, we will naturally try to form our school community in ways that support the feeling-will as much as the sense-nerve human being. Any resistance to shifting the balance towards the feeling-will has only one source: a dependence on the sense-nerve way of being. Not infrequently, attempts to promote the merits of the feeling-will evoke hostility. On the surface a fear of anarchy is projected onto the feeling-will when in fact the deeper source of resistance is the fear of letting go of the familiar sense-nerve in order to develop the feeling-will.

As teachers and parents we face the conventional pressures of our time to prepare our children for the "real world." But what is the real world? The global technological corporate world is certainly not going to disappear overnight. But are we clear with ourselves and parents about our pedagogical intent: to prepare our children to be successful in the world as it is at present and to prepare them to transform the world in the light of their true individuality and humanity?

Education is evolving. Rudolf Steiner has given us a conceptual framework for grasping the spiritual evolution of human consciousness. Steiner has given us practical indications, both in content and form, for how the education of children can best be achieved in the light of human evolution. Steiner did not merely offer educational ideals or theory, he tried to incarnate his insights into actual schools—mainly in Stuttgart and only a hand-full of others in his lifetime. Steiner was not only a thinker, he was an artist. He designed buildings such as the Goetheanum buildings, and like a true artist he was the most critical of their limitations. He saw how his creations could be improved upon and developed further. Just as the Goetheanum impulse is larger than the two buildings he created with that name, likewise the Waldorf impulse is more than the educational content and methods that go by that name today. The Waldorf impulse for education is alive where it is evolving and dying where it becomes fixed in content and/or form.

Inevitably, more and more schools will appear that in one way or another are touched by the Waldorf impulse for education but where in fact the deeper currents and vision manifest in diluted or distorted forms. This cannot be avoided entirely. It is not possible to keep the Waldorf movement pure. Trying to protect the names Waldorf and Steiner may in fact be a distraction for those whose wills are to deepen and extend the Waldorf impulse in order to meet the evolving needs of the children incarnating now and in the future. There is an increasing tension between the quantitative and qualitative growth of the Waldorf impulse in education. Some teachers are prepared to accept compromises believing that even an imperfect manifestation of the Waldorf impulse must reach as many children as possible. There is another equally persuasive view that some sacrifice of quantitative growth may be necessary in order that the Waldorf impulse can mature and deepen in the light of the long-term spiritual task of education. Each individual must decide for himself which impulse he feels called to serve. Some may be able to do both, but if not, there is honor in both directions.

In either case, concerning ourselves with the larger and long-term issues of human evolution which are central to the Waldorf impulse is directly related to serving the needs of the children of the present. The children before us today need to experience adults who consciously expand themselves beyond present reality, who actively devote themselves to creating the future through striving to develop new capacities. This brings us to consider the ways parents and teachers can educate their wills as an essential part of educating the wills of their children.

CHAPTER 3

Common Will and Comprehensive Will

In Chapter 1 we considered the development of free and authentic individuality as the primary goal of education. We saw that cognitive subjects challenge students to develop will in their thinking, while arts and crafts require that they learn to think in their willing. In both cases, it is through the inner effort made in exercising will-in-thinking and thinking-in-will that develops their spirit-will, their spirit individuality. In Chapter 2 we saw that most subjects, including arts and crafts, are taught in ways that exercise the sense-nerve human being while leaving the feeling-will under-developed. In our aspiration to educate whole human beings, we must reckon with the fact that we are at the beginning of learning how to develop feeling-will in our students. In Chapter 4 we will consider more fully the practical ways we can develop feeling-will in children appropriate to their stage of development from kindergarten through high school. Before doing so we have reason to look more deeply at teacher development.

I speak of teacher development, instead of teacher training, to emphasis the on-going, life-long development of the teacher as compared to what is possible in a two-year teacher training. Also, I wish to underscore the self-directed process of inner transformation compared to the outwardly acquired knowledge of child development and the content and methods of the curriculum.

> You can only become good teachers and educators if you pay attention not merely to what you do, but also to what you are. It is really for this reason that we have Spiritual Science with its anthroposophical outlook: to perceive the significance of the fact that man is effective in the world not only through what he does, but above all through what he is.
>
> We must above all become conscious of this first of educational tasks: that we must first make something of ourselves, so that a relationship in thought, an inner spiritual relationship, may hold sway between the teacher and the children.

— Rudolf Steiner, Stuttgart, August 21, 1919
(Lecture 1 in *Study of Man*)

Spiritual science expands our understanding of what it means to "make something of ourselves." Through the content of Steiner's *Theosophy* and other lectures, we learn about the transformation of our astral body into spirit self. If such thoughts seem abstract it is because they seem outside the parameters of what we can integrate meaningfully into our lives. However, in time a practical understanding of spirit self can give our everyday life and work purpose and direction. It can become the foundation for our ongoing development as teachers.

Children know experientially, unconsciously, which adults are working on themselves and which are not. "Making something of ourselves" becomes more concrete, and thus more practical, when we can grasp what it means to develop spirit self. In transforming our astral body we develop our authentic individuality (in contrast to our personality). However modest and inadequate our efforts may be, it is the development of our individuality through transforming our astral body that influences our children more profoundly than anything we say or do. In working upon our selves, our children are given a living model of developing individuality that awakens their own budding individuality.

In addition, it is through the transformation of our astral bodies that we develop the capacity to perceive moral imaginations regarding our work with the children. In this respect, the transformation of our astral bodies, the transformation of our own unfree thoughts, feelings and will impulses, is the key discipline for the art of education. For example, we can transform our natural tendency to act out of subjective sympathy and antipathy into a new capacity: to attend to the qualities of a child's outer appearance and behavior and through this discipline develop the eyes to see the child's soul and spirit individuality.

The significance of developing spirit self for our work is brought into focus through the following three sentences:

"Each epoch must...prepare, bear within it in a preparatory stage, what is to come in the ensuing period of culture."

"In the sixth epoch, it is the spirit self that must be developed within the souls of men, just as now the consciousness soul is being developed."

"The whole purpose of spiritual science is to prepare . . . for the sixth epoch of culture."

— Rudolf Steiner, *Preparing for the Sixth Epoch*
Dusseldorf, June 15, 1915

Towards finding a meaningful relationship to these thoughts, we might reflect on the fact that in the fourth cultural epoch individuals such as Plato and Aristotle, through their writing and work with students, cultivated a way of thinking that prepared for the scientific culture of our era, the fifth cultural epoch. In a comparable way, the sixth epoch will be a culture grounded in spiritual science that must be prepared by individuals today dedicated to developing spiritual faculties and capacities. Today the consciousness soul is being developed through mainstream culture. In anthroposophical and Waldorf circles our challenge is twofold: we must be grounded in the consciousness soul culture of our time while at the same time cultivate the first seeds of a spirit self culture. We can do this mostly through our individual effort to transform the unfree elements of our astral bodies and what we do subsequently out of our transformed capacities. We have no reason to be disheartened if our efforts appear to be quite modest in scope and effect.

There are two realms where we can see how the mastering of our astral bodies has practical implications. The first, as we have seen, is to better serve the children through the quality of our educational activities with them. There is much for us as educators to clarify and elaborate regarding the transforming of our unfree thinking, feeling and willing, without which our theory of child development and methods become lifeless husks. New forms of teacher development, both introductory and on-going, will surely emerge if we see the need to deepen the foundations of teacher development. To ensure that the Waldorf impulse for education does not atrophy but grows more vital we must concern ourselves with the ways each discipline can cultivate living thinking and creative willing. To make the inner shift from trying to standardize "best practices" to fostering a more individualized deepening of the Waldorf impulse challenges us to cultivate our spirit-will. From this perspective there is an urgent need for time and resources to be dedicated towards the spiritual deepening of introductory and on-going teacher development.

As the work with the children provides the primary impulse for self-transformation, our work with faculty, staff and parents surely provides the second impetus. Colleagues never cease to amaze and bewilder us by how differently they think, feel and will. Life would be so much simpler if our colleagues would only see the light of day and think, feel and will as we do! But apparently life is not meant to be so simple or easy, for the very diversity that frustrates and annoys us is quite obviously an act of God. Our problems with each other lie not in our differences, but in our own lack of insight and spiritual strength to recognize the complementary nature of our different ways of seeing and doing things. Only the limitations of our spirit-will prevent us from finding creative solutions that incorporate rather than suppress our diverse views and gifts.

In this context, the development of spirit self may be seen as a practical necessity rather than a remote possibility. The very existence of a school, its ability to function and survive on a day to day basis, depend on the ability of the faculty, staff and parents to work together. It is in the practical spheres of a school community that we meet in our will—my will, your will. The practical survival of any contemporary community depends on our capacity to direct our will in creative rather than destructive directions. If we want our communities to be shaped by creative rather than destructive will, we must make clear what causes will to become destructive rather than creative. Towards this end we will need to discern the kinds of will that shape community and institutional life. In particular, we must distinguish between "common will" and "comprehensive will."

In Lecture 5 of *The Social Future*, given in Zurich, October 24-30, 1919, Rudolf Steiner introduces the new concept of "comprehensive will" as distinct from the more familiar "common will." Steiner describes three types of society founded on three distinct expressions of will. He refers to past societies, such as monarchies, as "power societies" that were legitimately built on the power of one individual leader as long as it was a "divine will" that worked through the "individual will." An echo of this form of social order still exists today in the way parents raise their children. In the early childhood years, it is generally considered necessary and good that parents establish clear parameters for their children of what is acceptable and unacceptable behavior. Parents and teachers assume the authority and thus the power to create a social order they believe to be in the best interests of their children. Most parents do not abuse their power. Their love for their children motivates them to exercise their individual will in ways that serve the welfare of their children rather than their own selfish ends. Perhaps in such experiences we can find a glimmer of how individual will serves a higher or divine will.

No matter how appropriate and successful such a social order is for a family with young children, as adolescence approaches, parents and teachers are tested in their ability to adapt to a "sea change" in the social order of home and school. When children bargain for this and that in their early years parents recognize that often they must not give in to them. Slowly and often painfully for the adults, such bargaining becomes more difficult to oppose as it becomes necessary for the child's development to think for himself and learn to act responsibly. Bargaining is an unavoidable developmental step in the biography of each child, recapitulating a comparable step in the biography of humankind.

Particularly in the last five hundred years, as societies around the globe have increasingly formed around commerce and trade (instead of agriculture), more and more people demand, often at great physical and psychological risk, the right of self-determination. Today the need to exercise individual will in shaping the quality and direction of one's life arises as an elemental force in almost every human heart. However, as soon as multiple individual wills come to expression we see the birth of bargaining and competition, with each individual asserting his will against the will of others. For this reason Steiner calls this form of society the "bargaining society," based on a "competitive will." Many societies continue to create social order through the authority of one or an elite few because they see widespread individual bargaining and competition as an anti-social force leading to social chaos. The history of the last few centuries has at its center the drama of honoring or repressing individuality. The rise of democratic values and legal processes originates in the commitment to foster individuality.

The recognition of individual rights and dignity cannot be underestimated or taken for granted. And yet it is not for lack of appreciation for what we have that a growing number of people find it increasingly difficult to accept the competition and bargaining aspects of democratic/capitalistic society. Especially as globalization makes this the only kind of society, the self-interest and greed that are legitimized by capitalistic values and facilitated through democratic processes are seen more and more transparently as destructive and anti-social. Like those who fought for democracy against all odds, many people today, from depths they can hardly fathom themselves, challenge the premise that we must accept this as the best human nature can hope for. Human hearts ache to develop their individual potential, not only for self-advancement and personal gain, but to better serve human physical, psychological and spiritual needs. Growing numbers of people aspire to build community based on the diversity of insights and gifts living in each individual.

Rudolf Steiner addresses this deep human longing when he speaks of a "communing society" founded on "comprehensive will." This is the society of the sixth cultural epoch, the culture of spirit self, when our task will be to build a society of Philadelphia (love of brother). The fact that we are some fifteen hundred years from the beginning of this cultural period is no cause for procrastination. The communing society will not arise by itself; it will become reality only if some human beings have the will to create such a society by beginning today to develop the faculties and capacities that will be needed tomorrow.

One primary capacity of the sixth cultural epoch will be the ability to enter into and work with the thinking and especially the will impulses of others very different from our own. Our challenge is to find the spirit-will to make such foreign thoughts and will impulses our own in order to work creatively with them. In the communing society social harmony and unity will be founded not on "common will" but on "comprehensive will."

In Waldorf circles, as elsewhere, there is much discussion about consensus as an essential means for making decisions in a faculty-run school. It may be helpful to consider two different kinds of consensus: "compromise consensus" and "comprehensive consensus." The first form is more familiar, because it is the consensus found wherever democratic values and processes are honored. In healthy democracies there is usually a balance of views and intentions requiring give and take in order for all sides to find "common ground" by which they arrive at a compromise course of action.

Compromise consensus appears to be a process that honors the views of each individual. In practice it is often a process by which individuals bargain and compete to have their own views and wills win the day. Often enough, the so-called consensus embodies almost completely the will of one or a few who are often the most adept at bargaining. Despite the inequity in this situation, at least something gets done by those whose wills prevail. When consensus is not the will of one, it is usually the will of none. We should not be surprised if frequently nothing comes from such decisions because the price we pay for everyone winning a concession or two is that everyone's will is lamed.

Compromise consensus is inadequate to the spiritual needs of our time because it does not allow individuals to exercise their full human potential. By contrast, "comprehensive consensus," founded on the cultivation of comprehensive will, does challenge our full humanity. Towards gaining a practical understanding of comprehensive will we will turn to the Social Ethic verse given by Rudolf Steiner to the artist Edith Maryon:

The healthy social life is found,
When in the mirror of each individual
The whole community finds its reflection,
And when in the community
The virtue of each individual is living.

This verse points to two complementary capacities to be cultivated by each individual:

    i) To become a mirror that selflessly reflects points of view that belong to the community as a whole;
    ii) To develop and offer one's individual gifts and capacities to the community.

Correspondingly, the community of individuals is challenged to create a space

    i) where all individual perspectives can be heard in order for the community as a whole to be visible;
    ii) and where the virtue and gifts of each individual can unfold.

The verse is a positive expression of these capacities, but it can be helpful to consider their negative manifestations. Both the individual and the community are diminished and become unhealthy when individuals

    i) do not reflect their truth, their carefully considered perspectives of the community as a whole;
    ii) do not develop and offer their gifts and capacities.

Likewise:

i) when the perspectives of colleagues are judged by some as irrelevant or unhelpful;
ii) when a community does not avail itself of individuals' gifts and capacities, either through failing to foster an atmosphere of encouragement or through actually obstructing individuals from contributing their gifts, the very best they have to offer.

How does every individual, not just those in executive positions, become a mirror for reflecting the community as a whole? How can a community form itself around the gifts and potentials of each individual? The answer is found in cultivating "comprehensive will." Comprehensive will involves knowing our own will—our truth and our gift—while at the same time expanding ourselves to embrace the very different perspectives and gifts of every other individual in our community.

It must be noted that comprehensive will is a capacity exercised by individuals in relation to other individuals. It will be realized in practice only when two or more are moved in freedom to work in this direction because it is their will to do so. Likewise, only individuals can obstruct the process of building community through comprehensive will. They can do it in two ways. The first is by asserting that it is too idealistic, beyond our actual capacities. The second is to claim to be doing it already. Both positions are half-truths. Rather than say comprehensive will is impossible or something we already do, it is possible to say that we are committed to the long, hard work of developing the insight and capacity to practice comprehensive will evermore.

The idea of comprehensive will first came to my attention through Pietro Archiati's book *From Christianity to Christ*. I wish to acknowledge my debt and gratitude to Archiati for the clarity with which he reveals the meaning and significance of comprehensive will:

> To form the comprehensive or total will it is necessary to affirm the individuality of each person, to create a shared, outer framework which allows all individual wills to mutually foster and advance each other. Of course this is a much harder undertaking than reducing everything to a single will. But easier is not better. Freedom is harder than unfreedom, but not worse.
>
> Individual will means the will of the true ego of every human being. This will alone is truly individual. Most people know what they wish, but seldom what they will. The individualization of the will, as a process of increasing consciousness, has nothing to do with the egotism of the lower ego—for this is not individual at all. We can recognize real individuality by its spiritual and intuiting character, which can, in turn, only be grasped by thinking.

Archiati points to two related aspects of comprehensive will, which can be seen to correspond to the twofold aspect of the Social Ethic verse. The first is to "affirm the individuality of each person, to create a shared framework which allows all individual wills to mutually foster and advance each other." He is clear that this is different and more difficult "than reducing everything to a single will," or in other words, a common will. The second aspect, on which the first seems dependent, is that each individual know "what they will," not merely "what they wish." He is clear that this individual will has nothing to do with the egotism of the lower ego, but rather our "real individuality."

We might be tempted to think the challenge to know our own will is the easier of the two challenges. To know what we want for ourselves and other people is both easy and commonplace. But to know our will, the will of our individuality, is neither easy nor commonplace. To myself and others I may appear to know exactly what I want, but if and when I recognize that I am compelled in what I want, I recognize that I am unfree in my will. Only when I create a free space in myself, where I am not inwardly compelled to think, feel or want, can I know that *I* think, *I* feel, *I* will.

In his *Philosophy of Freedom* Rudolf Steiner gives the name "ethical individuality" to that in us that perceives moral imaginations and intuitions by which we can exercise free will. We can recognize ethical individuality in ourselves and others by the intuitive and creative character of thinking and actions. Ethical individualities know what they will.

But we might well ask how do ethical individualities work *together*? They see little merit in compromise consensus, not because they are too self-absorbed to be bothered, but because they seek another way of working with others. Those striving to work out of ethical individuality seek to meet the ethical individuality in the other. They do not try to persuade or bargain. Ethical individuals try to create a shared framework that will mutually foster each other's individuality. Ethical individuals seek a republican, not a democratic process; they aspire to exercise comprehensive consensus, not compromise consensus; they strive to exercise a comprehensive will, not a common will.

Some think our social problems originate in the fact that our egos are too big, that our sense of individuality is too strong. This perspective sees the need to repress individual will in ourselves and others in order to allow a common will to emerge as the basis for social harmony. Self-will and egotism are obstacles to social life that must be reckoned with. But egotism can manifest in subtle ways, for example, in the claim to have no personal agenda. To have no agenda is to not know our will. If we do not know our will, our task is to develop our individuality so that we can know our will. In our time and in our circles, such claims may express a failure in self-knowledge or a disingenuous ploy. In either case, the fact that our will remains a hidden agenda, perhaps even to ourselves, makes self-will and egotism all the more insidious and anti-social.

To have an agenda is not only unavoidable, it is essential to social life. As we have seen, the healthy social life requires that we know and represent our perspectives and develop our gifts. It appears that we have a love/hate relationship to individuality. We want to be individuals ourselves and claim to support others in unfolding their individuality, but at the same time we demonstrate a deep-seated distrust of individuality, quick to equate it with egotism. In Waldorf and anthroposophical circles we have a wealth of conceptual resources on this matter and yet there is little evidence that we avail ourselves of such insights in the social principles and methods presently in vogue in our circles. Our attachment to consensus processes in which we attempt to establish a *common* vision and a *common* will as the foundation to our institutional and community life does not appear to take fully into account present and future development of human individuality.

Rudolf Steiner gives us the following perspective of human development that is both humbling and inspiring:

From the last third of the nineteenth century (1879) the situation has been completely reversed. The spirits of light who have been continuing in their activities have done enough where the establishment of blood, tribal, racial and similar bonds is concerned, for everything has its time in evolution. In the general and rightful scheme of things, enough has been done to establish what needed to be established through blood bonds in humanity. In more recent times, therefore, the spirits of light have changed their function. They now inspire human beings to develop independent ideas, feelings and impulses for freedom; they now make it their concern to establish the basis on which people can be independent individuals. And it is gradually becoming the task of the spirits who are related to the old spirits of darkness to work within the blood bonds.

— Rudolf Steiner, *Spirits of Light and Spirits of Darkness,* Dornach, October 26, 1917

The spiritual perspective Steiner offers reveals why political nationalism and religious fundamentalism based on bonds of common blood, culture and religion are increasingly a source of destructive forces. The full implications of Steiner's perspective, however, are not limited to the obvious extremes we see in the world today. *Not just common blood, but all attempts to reduce diversity to commonality and uniformity are threats to the rightful unfolding of human individuality.* The spiritual drama Steiner describes is present wherever social unity and harmony are sought through outer policies, regulations and laws based on "common values" to which all individuals are expected to submit. The spiritual forces working through consumerism, corporatism, and institutionalism may have nothing to do with blood ties, but they too are vehicles through which human individuality is assaulted. With this in mind we have reason to pause: to what extent are we in our own institutions repressing the legitimate unfolding of individuality, our own as much as that of colleagues? To what extent does this threaten the long-term viability of the very thing we intend to serve, namely, the education of our children and the evolution of human culture and society?

We are good people, as are the experts we consult to help us to meet the complexities of institutional life. But the spiritual realities and challenges of our time place before each individual and each community of individuals the question:

"Am I, are you, seeking community through a spirit of commonality or individuality? Do I, do you, aspire to build community through common will or comprehensive will?"

This question is not one we need take up as an agenda item for decision. There is no reason to persuade our colleagues that this is how "we" should work together. There is certainly nothing to bargain over in order to arrive at a consensus. We can do this without saying a word to anyone. We need no mandate from anyone but ourselves to direct our will towards cultivating comprehensive will in any circumstance.

At the same time, this is something we have every reason to discuss with colleagues, both formally and informally. There is every reason to help each other grow into this new potential for our work together. We will need to be generous towards each other regarding our limitations to practice comprehensive will. But as individuals we need to be clear with ourselves and then with our colleagues about the difference and significance of cultivating common will compared with comprehensive will. We are at a fork in the road. The path we choose matters very much. It matters that some educators make a conscious decision to cultivate comprehensive will and comprehensive consensus as their guiding principles for building community. It will better serve the development of our children by better serving our own development. It is also true to the cultural evolution that the Waldorf impulse for education embraces and serves.

If fully grasped, the perspectives of this chapter can easily add to our sense of burden. Rather than lightening our burden by marginalizing or dismissing these views, one additional thought may give them meaning. In Lecture 4 of *Study of Man* Steiner describes the seven types or levels of will:

Physical – instinct		Spirit Man – resolve
Etheric – impulse/drive	Ego – motive	Life Spirit – intention
Astral – desire		Spirit Self – wish to
		do better

Recently, the otherwise abstract quality of such a list unexpectedly came alive for me as a kind of revelation. This occurred when I noted that in reference to spirit self, Rudolf Steiner did not merely say, "wish" but rather, "wish to do better." With every sculpture I make, every course or lecture I give, every article I write, I am left with the feeling that it is not as good as it could be. I wish I could do it better. The revelation was that in the moment I observe myself wishing to do something better, I am conscious of my spirit self not in abstraction but in living reality.

Whenever we find the spark of will to do better, to become freer in ourselves, we can find strength in knowing our spirit self is stirring from potential towards actual reality. And where two or more come together in the spirit-will to do better, surely we are building, if not a road, perhaps a footpath to Philadelphia.

CHAPTER 4

Educating the Will in Practice

In Chapters 1-3 we began to clarify our understanding of the nature and development of the will. If there is any topic on which we cannot stop at mere understanding it is surely the education of the will. From the beginning we have established that we must learn to perceive will if we are to know it in reality, not merely in theory. Everything that is said about will must be rooted in perception and thus confirmed, modified or elaborated more fully through subsequent perceptions. For example, we have observed that raw will is a force that moves our limbs and makes things happen, but by itself it only wreaks havoc, chaos and destruction. At the very least we must exercise thinking in order to give form and direction to our limbs. To exercise and develop will, our own as much as our students, our actions must be guided by insight. What at first may seem abstract theory can in time lead to a capacity to perceive directly. The descriptions about will given in Chapters 1-3 are like a map of a foreign land. The map is not the actual place but with one, however sketchy or imperfect it may be, we have a better chance of finding our way than with no map at all. In this last chapter, with map in hand, we now enter the actual landscape where we educate the will in practice.

In Chapter 2 we considered some practical examples, in particular, two different ways to carve a spoon. The two approaches arose in relation to two different pedagogical intents: to develop "thinking-will" or "feeling-will." In this chapter we will expand on this, looking at additional projects that span the full spectrum of schooling from kindergarten through high school. What is offered here is not intended to be definitive or complete. Some examples are elaborated more fully, while others are mere indications. In either case, these examples are offered as starting points in the assumption that each individual will find his own relationship to them and hopefully develop them further. Although the emphasis is on the visual arts, in particular sculpture, the intention is to stimulate teachers working in all media to consider the deeper developmental significance of their disciplines. I hope some will recognize the need to adapt their ways of working in the various arts and crafts in order to serve the development of different kinds of will. It is too simplistic to regard the arts and crafts as "educating the will" in comparison to the development of thinking through academic subjects. To educate the will truly and fully we must refine our perceptions and our practical methods to be in tune with the more subtle and diverse nature of will.

A primary purpose of this book is to clarify conceptually and practically the distinction between two very different yet complementary forms of will. The first, more widely understood and practiced, I call "thinking-will," more commonly called "head and hand co-ordination." The second is not so well understood or cultivated; I call it "feeling-will" or we might call it "head, heart and hand co-ordination." In fact, we have hardly begun the task of developing this side of human will. Because the development of the feeling-will is a new frontier, where there is the greatest need for developing appropriate methods, I will consciously emphasize this aspect in the practical examples that follow. With several projects I will continue the method of describing two contrasting approaches, in part to affirm that there is always more than one way. However, more significantly, I place the more familiar "thinking-will" approach next to that of the "feeling-will" in order to emphasis the qualitative distinctions between the two. Without intending any slight towards developing "thinking-will," my unabashed hope is to inspire more teachers to concern themselves with the development of "feeling-will" in their students.

We have good reason to turn to Steiner and others for guidance and inspiration, but it contradicts an essential activity of the educator to seek prescriptions and recipes that detail every aspect of when, what, and how to do projects. Above all else, each teacher must stand before his or her students as a model of striving individuality, rather than as a pedagogical automaton. That does not mean that we should go to the other extreme and do only what suits us personally. Our service to our children can be sidetracked in two directions: by working only according to our own inclinations or by seeking the one-and-only right way. Our individuality is exercised and can thereby serve as a living model for the children when we strive to intuit which project and method we should bring to our students. By continuing automatically to do what we did before out of personal habit or a preconceived notion of the "one right way," we side step our own authentic ego activity. By developing the inner strength to sustain equanimity in the face of doubt and uncertainty we exercise our own spirit-will.

If we work in a "thinking-will" manner merely because it is our preferred way of working and/or because we think it is the only way to work, then we do so automatically, thus avoiding doubt and uncertainty. Holding back such automatic inclinations is the pre-requisite for awakening the intuitive capacity of our feeling-will. Feeling-will is a new capacity that is not exercised automatically; it requires active spirit-will. If we can see the merit of strengthening the spirit-will of our children through exercising their feeling-will, then we will see the need to cultivate it in ourselves. As we awaken to our own feeling-will, whole new horizons will open before us as to how we can serve the unfolding of our children's full humanity.

KINDERGARTEN:

The defining characteristic of feeling-will is the capacity to live deeply into the inner quality of something outside us, knowing and feeling it as if we are within it or it is within us. In the early childhood years a healthy child is naturally inclined to drink in the inner mood and qualities of place and person. It is one of the trag-edies of our times that the ways of the world, including the life of family and school, can dullen rather than foster this natural soul attunement. Tragically, many young children come to kindergarten with a sense-nerve disposition already strongly developed. Their thinking is prematurely intellectual and abstract, and their feeling life inclines toward strong personal like or dislike. It is crucial for later life that in these early years we do everything we can to keep the feeling-will alive as much and as long as possible.

In early childhood we do not "teach" the arts and crafts to the children so much as we create opportunities for children to be exposed to and engage in the realm of art as a natural part of every-day life. We can do this in a variety of ways.

1. One way to foster the artist in each child is to provide frequent opportunities for engaging in art and craft activity. The following are just some possibilities to consider:

    a) A natural clay pit, such as can be found at the edge of a stream, within walking distance of the kindergarten, is a wonderful gift from Mother Nature. If we can overcome any personal aversion we may have to clay and the so-called mess it can create, then the children can reap the full benefit of her gift. Allowing our children to "muck about" to their hearts' and wills' content, without inter-jecting cautionary admonitions, is a true and lasting gift we can give them. Their souls' receptivity to the elemen-tary quality of matter, to the spirit of the elementals and Mother Nature, is a precious capacity that can fade all too soon. By enduring a little mess, we give our children experiences in heart and will which are a source of health and strength for a lifetime.

    b) In the absence of the good fortune of having a natural clay pit nearby, we can create one for the children to seek out in free play. Dig a hole a foot deep and two feet in diameter and fill it with at least one hundred pounds of clay. A bucket of clay indoors available for free play is also desirable.

    c) In addition to outdoor sandboxes, we can also create a sandbox for free-play indoors. With a sheet of plywood and some 1″x 4″ or 1″x 6″ pine, we can make a 3′x 6′ or 4′x 8′ sandbox with sides or legs of appropriate height.

The developmental value of moving and shaping sand is so important that its use should not be limited by the seasons but be possible year round. Snow is a wonderful material as well but does not replace sand as a form-building medium. See Fig. 5, below.

Fig. 5. Indoor sandbox

d) We can use earthtone beeswax for modeling with the children. All materials have color—natural beeswax has a golden earthtone color. But as educators we have good reason to be sensitive to the different effects produced by modeling a material that has strong color—primary and secondary colors—in contrast to one with earthtones. Can we distinguish between a deeply felt color experience and a deeply felt form experience?

In finger-painting, for example, children have a tactile experience that competes with and may over-ride their color experience. Likewise, the strong color experience of brightly colored beeswax interferes with a vivid form experience. This is even more pronounced when children assemble beeswax figures from part to whole, using several different bright colors of wax.

To become fully engaged and absorbed in something means to give our whole heart and mind to it. Here the distinction between color experience and form experience is also related to the distinction between sense-nerve and feeling-will experience. When we give children brightly colored beeswax, however good our intentions, we are exposing them to two different worlds at the same time. If we want them to develop a capacity to live deeply into form, we want to minimize rather than maximize the color experience during modeling. The use of simple, natural-colored beeswax allows the child to have a pure form experience, which strengthens the feeling-will.

e) Provide sunflower seeds, corn kernels, rice or other grains and let the children draw and create patterns with them on a large surface.

Unlike drawing on paper, this allows them to move and change the forms so that, for example, a tree turns into a bird. See Fig. 6. The seeds also lend themselves to creating non-outline forms—outline forms are the result of sense-nerve experience, while the filled-out forms allow the feeling-will to be active. See Fig. 7 on the next page.

Figs. 6 a and b. A tree transforms into a bird.

Figs. 7 a, b, and c. Simple transformation

Figs. 7 d and e. Trees

f) Provide good rasps that allow the children to rasp to
their hearts' content. Sawing logs and hammering pieces
of wood together with nails is a great favorite, but is

largely a sense-nerve experience. Rasping and rubbing sticks and/or corncobs against softer wood inspire a more feeling-will creative play. Little children do not need to be making anything specific, unless their own imagination spontaneously sees something like an animal—it is natural that what they see in the form will change and evolve as they work.

g) There is every reason to have stone and stone tools in the playground as well. Limestone and marble are not too hard. An old, not-so-sharp hatchet or roofer's hammer is a good tool. Again, children do not need a preconceived idea of what they are making, nor do they need verbal instruction in how to use the tool. All that matters is that the children have the freedom to chip away, that the free play of their limbs communes unconsciously with the beauty of the material—they will covet the sparkling chips as precious treasures. In terms of safety precautions it is sufficient that we are quietly present nearby, provide safety goggles, and allow only one child at a time to work.

The above suggestions are just a starting point and stimulus for early childhood educators to become more open to the potential of all manner of materials that may be readily available and can serve this vital need of the children to engage in formative activity. The list of activities is limited only by our openness to the possibilities, yet the point is not for every kindergarten to have every possible material on hand. These few examples are intended to bring into focus developmental considerations that can influence our choice of activities and how we provide them to the children.

It is important to note that all the above examples are for free play. I have made no reference to doing beeswax or painting as formal activities guided by the teacher. It is generally understood that we are not teaching painting or beeswax but are simply creating opportunities for the children to enter into these realms of experience. However, we can gain a fuller perspective on the distinction between guiding and teaching if we consider ourselves as creative workers in the kindergarten rather than as teachers.

2. To appreciate a second way of fostering the artistic in the kindergarten, we need to examine a common assumption derived from mainstream culture, namely, that only a gifted few are artistic and creative with their hands. The culture of anthroposophy would have us see it otherwise, namely, that being artistic is not simply a profession or vocation but a way of being human. There is an artist in each one of us that is integral to our humanity. Mainstream culture and education are founded on the perception that there is a potential scientist in each human being that must be developed for the benefit of both the individual and society. Many of us may not think of ourselves as scientists in the professional sense—we may not be particularly good at science—but our education and most forms of work nevertheless call upon the scientist or bureaucrat in us. Likewise, we may not think of ourselves as artists—we may not be particularly artistic—nevertheless, education can develop the potential artist in each of us. Indeed, this artist in us is our other half, the complement to the scientist in us. Our own wholeness as human beings depends on our cultivating the way of perceiving, thinking and acting of both the scientist and artist that are complementary sides of our human nature. The wholeness of our children depends on our ability as parents and teachers to be living models of the striving to develop and harmonize the artist and the scientist within us.

With the above perspective we can appreciate the great gift we give our children when as teachers and parents we work creatively with our hands on a regular basis. A holy mood surrounds all authentic artistic activity, but it need not be extraordinary. Put another way, artistic activity is the extraordinary in ordinary everyday life.

If we aspire to foster each child's artistic potential and his feeling-will nature in particular, then it is essential that we embody this feeling-will nature ourselves. Towards this end, it is important that we, as much as the children, have a variety of materials and tools always on hand, so that we can take up creative work as the spirit moves us. For us adults there are two main obstacles to overcome. If we have little experience with or natural inclination toward working creatively with our hands, it is understandable that we may be shy, if not anxious, about beginning to do so in front of the children and other adults. In this case, our love for the children, and our good will to do whatever it takes to serve their developmental needs, will motivate us. If they need us to be creative doers, then surely we can find a way to make a modest beginning. If we simply begin, our skill and love for creative work will grow over time.

Whether we are at home working creatively or not, a second stumbling block can arise through the inner shift we must make from "teacher mode" to "worker mode." To become inwardly engaged in some work activity we must be able to step out of the teacher role, where we may be primarily or exclusively watching out for the children's safety and other practical considerations. Of course, we cannot abandon these responsibilities for a personal creative "fling." It is, nonetheless, possible to keep an eye out for looming disasters without coming out of the absorption in our creative work except as necessity demands it. Where there are two adults, it is possible for one to maintain the teacher role so that the other adult can enter more freely into creative activity for an extended period.

The biggest obstacle, however, is our own inertia, that delights in anything—such as the need to attend to the children—that will relieve us from engaging our creative will. The inner shift from "teacher mode" to "worker mode" can also be expressed in the shift from our "sense-nerve" to our "feeling-will" nature. Entering and sustaining a feeling-will consciousness is no small challenge for us in today's sense-nerve existence, with telephones, faxes, email and cars increasingly dominating our lives. We have much to be grateful for in today's world, but the way of life it has created is out of balance. A world of limitless technological conveniences does not meet our own need or that of our children to become whole human beings. For our children to glimpse the activity of our creative spirit in spheres of matter, however imperfect, is as important to their future health and potential as the elemental experience of Mother Nature mentioned earlier.

3. We can also provide original works of art and craft in the kindergarten. Prints of great paintings such as Raphael's *Sistine Madonna* serve one need; original paintings or sculptures serve another. An original work created by a teacher, parent or artist, even if it is not a great work of art, is a tangible embodiment of creative spirit that a print or copy is not. Ideally, every kindergarten would have an original painting, mural or sculpture created by a teacher or local artist. If it can be created on site, the children have not only the gift of a finished original work of art but in addition they imbibe the living spirit of the creative process. Using cups and plates, vases, picture frames and other practical things for daily use that have been crafted by hand instills a deep sense that creative spirit has its place in all domains of human life.

4. There is a fourth area of artistic activity that can supplement the teacher's regular creative activity. Local artists and craftpeople are a resource to be drawn upon more fully. Often there are parents or friends of friends who are stonecarvers, woodcarvers, blacksmiths, weavers and other craftpeople who could be invited to work on campus once or twice a week for a few hours over a period of weeks. An artist- or craftsperson-in-residence, permanently or at least for a whole school year, would be even more desirable.

Of course, it requires real vision and understanding to see that such creative adult activity in the children's surroundings during these most impressionable early years is well worth the small price it requires in terms of physical and financial resources. It is simply a matter of our values and the priorities we derive from our values. If one of our central educational values is to develop whole human beings then we must ensure that our children interact on a daily basis with individuals who exemplify feeling-will.

FIRST THROUGH FIFTH GRADE:

Form Modeling
The very first lesson a Waldorf class teacher gives on the first day of the First Grade is traditionally the drawing of the straight line and curved line. Through this simple but profound beginning the teacher and the children embark on their eight-year odyssey together. This introduction to the language of line sets the tone of artistic perception and experience that underlies all subjects in the lower school. It also launches the years of Form Drawing that is so central to the Waldorf curriculum.
There is much to discover in straight and curved lines, not least of which is that straight and curve are as fundamental to the

world we inhabit as red, yellow and blue. But straightness and cur-
vature do not manifest only as line. Everywhere we look we see
natural and man-made forms consisting of flat and curved, convex
and concave surfaces. Form is as primary as color; flat and curved
surfaces are as fundamental as straight and curved lines. Given this
fact, we might ponder why we do not introduce our children to the
world of flat and curved surfaces parallel to our introducing the
world of straight and curved lines. Form Modeling should be as
integral a part of the lower school curriculum as is Form Drawing.

For this to come about class teachers must awaken to the
vital importance of engaging the children in the tactile world of
wavy *surfaces* as much as wavy lines. With a clear and deep commitment, we discover a whole new discipline opening before us. All
that Steiner gave us in regards to Form Drawing can serve as a foundation upon which we can build the elements of a Form Modeling
curriculum through the grades. The suggestions that follow are a
mere beginning, drawn from the efforts of a few Waldorf artists and
educators over the last few years. They are offered in the hope of
inspiring all lower-school teachers to take up this important discipline and develop it further.

Seed Drawing

One starting point is to work in a medium that stands between the two dimensions of drawing and the three dimensions of
modeling. In the section on the kindergarten we saw the possibility
of free play with grains such as sunflower seeds, rice, corn kernels
and such. Such materials also lend themselves to drawing any and
all line forms normally done with paper and crayon. For example,
each child can make a straight line, beginning with only two seeds
placed on opposite sides of his desk. They can then add a third in

the middle between the first two, and then two more, and so on. This introduces possibilities that drawing does not afford. The line incarnates gradually from a non-physical to physical reality—ideally the grains never touch, so that the line is visible without being physically solid. Inevitably, their straight line will be a little curved, wavy or wobbly. The best part is that we can move one or another grain to make it straighter. We can then make a second line that is curved, or we can also transform the original straight line into an intentional curve. Once we try these basic starting points, both teacher and students will hardly be able to contain themselves as other possibilities present themselves. See Fig. 8 below.

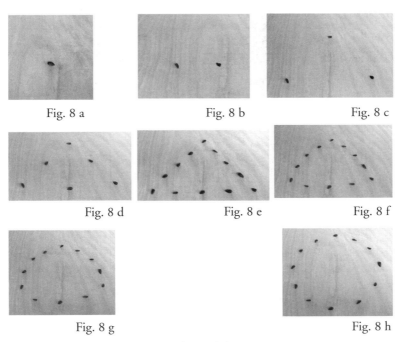

Fig. 8 a   Fig. 8 b   Fig. 8 c

Fig. 8 d   Fig. 8 e   Fig. 8 f

Fig. 8 g   Fig. 8 h

Figs. 8 a-h. Seed drawing

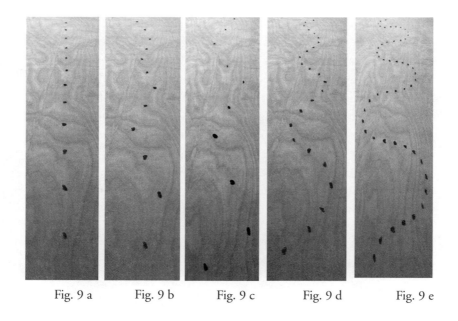

| Fig. 9 a | Fig. 9 b | Fig. 9 c | Fig. 9 d | Fig. 9 e |

Figs. 9 a-e. Building-up a meander form

The other wonderful potential of Seed Drawing is that it is easily adapted from an individual to a group activity. A whole class could do Seed Drawing on the floor or on a couple of sheets of plywood set on top of their desks. Start with each child placing one seed to make one straight line together—no small accomplishment. Then move them out of a straight line into a wavy line. Add more seeds to make the wavy line more visible and adjust it to make it as flowing and harmonious as possible. Gradually, transform the wavy line into a free and dynamic meander form. From such a beginning many other group forms can be created. See Fig. 9 a–f.

Fig. 9 f. A dynamic meander form

Sand Modeling

Seed Drawing is just that, drawing. It is three-dimensional only insofar as the seeds have volume, but the forms we make are essentially two-dimensional. To enter the world of three dimensions, other media are better suited. Moist sand offers such potential. A sandy beach or large outdoor sandbox can be used if available. Otherwise, plastic bins with lids can be bought or wooden boxes can be made—16"x 24" and 4–6 inches deep works well. The plastic containers with lids are very handy for storing on top of each other but they can crack and break from regular use. Wooden boxes should be varnished; otherwise they will warp and rot from the water in the sand. The weight of such sandboxes and the inevitable spilling of sand on the floor are factors that may inhibit us, but the conviction that sand modeling is essential can motivate us to be undeterred by such inconveniences.

Fig.10. From formless chaos to quiet flatness in sand

Prepare the sand by adding the right amount of water, neither too much nor too little. The children can then be shown how to mix and sift with loving care to ensure that the sand is the right consistency throughout. From this starting point, the teacher demonstrates how to slowly redistribute the sand and with a light touch to level it into a flat surface. Try to find a harmonious motion for the children to imitate—no pounding. As you create this flat surface, build up a simple but vivid imagination of a great expanse of water or a flat desert to help the children awaken to a feeling experience of flatness that is not bound by the physical limitation of the sandbox. Do not rush; dare to push the envelope of staying in this world of flatness as long as you think the children can manage. Our aim is to bring each child into the feeling experience of flatness for a sustained period. See Fig. 10 above.

This feeling experience of flatness will be further enhanced if we transform the flatness into a slight mound or a convex, curved surface. We do it in a manner that draws attention to the slightest curving up of the whole area, so that we—and the children—stay in the transformative process as opposed to jumping to a finished result. If possible, go back and forth between a slight bulging and flattening and bulging again, in order that the contrasting feelings of flattening and bulging intensify. Having created a convex curve, return to the flat surface and then create a slight hollowed-out concave surface. Go back and forth between flat and concave, even concave and convex, so that the children learn to dwell in these three different surfaces of convex/flat/concave, and in their corresponding feelings of expanding life/quiet stillness/open receptivity. See Fig. 11 below.

Fig. 11. Convex/Concave

It is not possible to elaborate here on this simple beginning, but where enthusiasm is kindled, further possibilities will present themselves. For example, it is natural to draw a line with our finger on a flat surface of moist sand. It is possible to start from a simple wavy line that gradually becomes a wavy surface by shifting from using a finger to using the palm of our hand. In this way any form done in form drawing can be adapted to sand modeling. See Fig. 12 on the next page.

Fig. 12 a.   Fig. 12 b.

Fig. 12 c.

Fig. 12 d.

Form Modeling in Clay

Clay modeling is not used as much as it might be in Waldorf schools. Some teachers find clay too cold and messy. This obstacle is compounded by the so-called pedagogical "principle" that clay is inappropriate before Third or Fourth Grade. Typically, clay modeling is used in the lower grades to supplement a main lesson theme— a story, man and animal, architecture, and so forth. We will look at this aspect of clay modeling after first considering another undeveloped potential of clay.

Clay can complement the use of sand as a medium for form modeling beginning in First Grade. Sand lends itself to making larger and more readily changed surfaces than clay; however, clay allows finer detail and more complexity than sand. For example, the children can build a one- to two-inch thick slab of clay that they must make as flat as possible. On this flat slab they can draw wavy and zigzag lines, and also more elaborate form drawings. The clay will create more resistance than the sand, yet will lend itself to more refinement. See Figs. 13 a-d below.

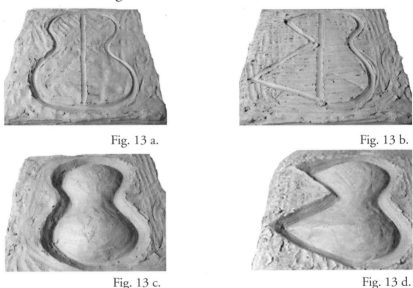

Fig. 13 a.

Fig. 13 b.

Fig. 13 c.

Fig. 13 d.

Clay can also be used like Seed Drawing, breaking off small pieces of clay to create straight, curved and other lines. With clay, as with seeds, it is possible to vary the width of the line. A line that fluctuates from wide to narrow is more dynamic than a line with a fixed width. Clay is especially suitable for bringing the two-dimensional forms into three dimensions—after varying the width, it is natural with clay to vary the height so that it flows from higher to lower. The questions of when and how to bring this according to the developmental stages of the children need to be researched as part of the overall elaboration of a Form Modeling curriculum. See Figs. 14 a–g.

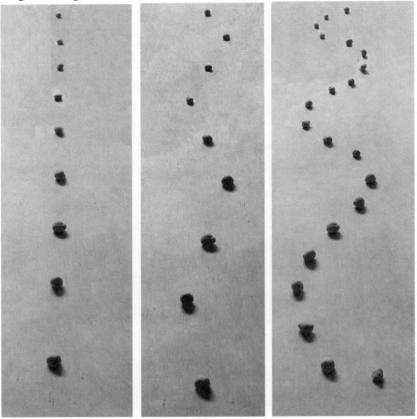

Fig. 14 a.   Fig. 14 b.   Fig. 14 c.

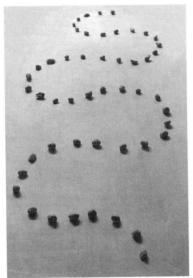

Fig. 14 d.

Fig. 14 e.

Fig. 14 f.

Fig. 14 g.

Modeling Human and Animal Forms

One important consideration for teachers to keep in mind when modeling in clay or any other material is the distinction between a feeling-will versus a sense-nerve way of modeling human, animal and even architectural forms. Take the example of building a pyramid or Greek temple in clay. It is, of course, historically correct to build up such structures stone by stone, but there is also reason to form them from a whole volume of clay, slowly moving the clay around to arrive gradually at the desired form. The pedagogical consideration for guiding the children in the one way over the other is the choice between exercising the children's thinking-will versus their feeling-will.

If this distinction is clear with regard to making buildings in clay, it should be all the more apparent when modeling human and animal forms. In this case, we have no reason for sculpting such living forms part by part when Mother Nature herself forms them organically, with every part growing out of and integral to the whole. It is important to understand the deeper reason for working from the whole; otherwise, working from the whole to the part becomes a cliché or formula. We work from the whole in order to create out of *gesture*. What is the reason for working out of gesture? Although we are making sculptures in a physical material such as clay, when we work out of gesture we are making not merely physical but etheric human or animal forms. We exchange the goal of realism for that of creating form gestures that are heavy or light, contracted or expansive, restful or active. See Fig.15 on the next page. In doing so, we awaken to more subtle feeling perceptions belonging to the forces of our etheric body and the etheric world. When we work organically, imbuing every part with the overall gesture of the whole, we are engaged in our feeling-will. In feeling-will or head/heart/hand activity, our etheric body mediates between the astral and physical.

When we work mechanically from fixed preconceptions and/or from personal sympathy and antipathy we are active in our sense-nerve side. In sense-nerve, thinking- will or head/hand activity, our astral body incarnates thought and feeling impulses directly into the physical without the mediation of etheric forces. *Here lies the deepest significance for exercising the feeling-will over the sense-nerve. It is nothing less than the difference between developing the perception and the capacity to work creatively within the living spirit of the etheric.* In sense-nerve activity the living archetypes of the astral world become spiritual husks of abstract thought when they are materialized without the mediation of etheric gesture.

Fig. 15. Human form as living gesture

This deeper perspective of the developmental significance of clay modeling and how we approach it can illuminate what is otherwise a source of confusion: what do we mean when speaking about working from the whole to the part? At first, it may seem like a simple matter, if all we mean is to form a human being from a single piece of clay or wax rather than making head and limbs separately and then joining them together. For all its simplicity, such a principle becomes fixed dogma if we employ it because "this is the way it is done in Waldorf schools." We can avoid artistic dogmatism when we know why we do things in one way rather than another. We hold a dogmatic position if we think that we must always work from a whole mound of clay or other material such as wood or stone and never build up with pieces of clay that gradually create a whole. In order to grasp the subtle complexities of the relationship between part and whole, we must have a vivid sense for the difference between a creative process permeated by etheric in contrast to astral forces, and how this underlies the distinction made here between a feeling-will and sense-nerve activity.

We have already seen with a project such as a spoon that we can carve a block of wood in an astral, sense-nerve manner or in an etheric, feeling-will manner. Likewise, we can build up from parts to whole, for example in clay, in either a sense-nerve or feeling-will manner. Making a human form by adding arms and legs and head to a torso is a sense-nerve process, whereas bringing out the limbs from a whole piece of clay is a feeling-will process. See Fig. 16. However, it is also quite possible to build up pieces of clay that gradually

Fig. 16. Two ways to create a human form—feeling-will in the three forms above and thinking-will in the form below

form the final whole through a feeling-will process. See Fig. 17. In fact, we do this when we do shaded drawing. Each stroke contributes to a whole that only gradually emerges. See Fig. 18. Similarly, we can build up pieces of clay to make three-dimensional forms in a feeling-will manner as in Fig. 14 above.

Fig. 17 a.

Fig. 17 b.

Fig. 17 c.

Figs. 17 a-c. Human form built up, piece by piece, out of feeling gesture

Figs. 18 a-b. Two circular surfaces— built up with strokes above and filled in outline below

We can work from a whole piece of clay or build up pieces towards a physical whole. The more decisive factor is whether we work in a thinking-will or a feeling-will manner. In Fig. 19 a we see an egg-like whole that is gradually differentiated into head and limbs. In Fig. 19 b a sphere is cut with a blade to create the surfaces of a tetrahedron (pyramid). Both are created from a physical whole but in the one case out of feeling- will while in the other out of think-ing-will. Likewise, it is possible to build up pieces of clay into a whole in either a thinking-will or a feeling-will manner. Fig. 20 shows two human figures built up from parts to whole. The lower figure is made from separate arms, legs and head stuck to-gether to make the whole. The upper fig-ure is built up with small pel-let-like pieces

Fig. 19 a. Transformation of whole in organic, feeling-will manner

that contribute to the gradual emergence of head and limbs. Whether we create the parts from the whole or build up parts into a whole, we can do so out of felt gesture. Such gestural feeling is permeated by the formative activity of the etheric. This living gesture by which we come into a more conscious experience of the etheric formative forces brings us to the deeper significance of exercising feeling-will.

Fig. 19 b. Transformation of whole in mechanical, thinking-will manner

Fig. 20. Two human forms built up with pieces—organic feeling-will above and mechanical thinking-will below

Stone Carving

Stone carving offers great potential in the lower grades. Stone carving can be offered as a course, such as soapstone carving, where the preceding discussion can help us see how to approach the process. In this context I mention it as an activity for free play, such as at recess. A recent experience has demonstrated that stone carving has a special appeal to children in Grades One through Three. Two years ago I carved an eight-foot block of Vermont marble as a memorial to Stephen Edelglass, the former high school physics teacher at Green Meadow Waldorf School in Spring Valley, NY. I spent six months carving it on site at the school. Not only were the children, teachers and parents able to watch the sculpture evolve from week to week, young and old alike were welcome to join in the actual carving. To see the First- and Second-Graders line up for months at every recess to take a turn carving was a great delight to everyone who witnessed it. I had a number of conversations with teachers and parents about how powerfully the stone carving spoke to the children of this age. It was obvious that the children need and seek such experiences. As our sense-nerve nature increasingly dominates our way of life, our children seek every opportunity to unfold the health giving forces of this other side of their feeling-will. Even without the active presence of a stonecarver, I am convinced that it is within the capacity of class teachers and/or parents to organize and monitor such creative will activities. What it would give the children to be able to carve a block of stone as part of their free play? What it would give to our children if, instead of seeing their teacher patrolling the school yard or chatting, they saw her or him pick up hammer and chisel and carve a block of stone or wood every day?

Woodcarving

By Fifth or Sixth Grade, if not before, woodcarving is traditionally added to the curriculum of a Waldorf school. Today, it is no small achievement to establish and sustain a woodcarving program. The social/economic forces of our time grow stronger every day, tempting even Waldorf schools to question the use of limited resources to provide the necessary tools, space and qualified teacher. One hope towards countering this trend is for parents and teachers to familiarize themselves with the very contemporary value of woodcarving. Woodcarving is not offered as a retreat from the technological advances of contemporary culture. When taken up with the appropriate insight, woodcarving provides children with opportunities to develop capacities directly relevant to the challenges of contemporary life.

When woodcarving in the lower school is discussed among teachers, the focus is usually on what projects to do and when to do them. It is generally understood that there is a "Waldorf way" to do things in every subject/discipline derived from Rudolf Steiner's insights into the developmental readiness of children at each grade level. Whether a school starts its woodcarving program in Sixth, Fifth or even Fourth Grade, there is a strong tradition in Waldorf schools to begin by making an egg, followed by a spoon, and at some point a bowl. Other projects such as picture frames, candleholders and movable toys are also done along the way. Despite developmental concerns about what and when to bring particular projects, the sequence of projects is in reality not so much based on the age of the children as on a natural progression of skill, on the one hand, and artistic experience on the other.

Generally speaking, it is only in Fourth or Fifth Grade that most children are ready to cultivate the dexterity and skill of rasping, whittling and carving. Most teachers feel intuitively, more than rationally, that there is some wisdom in starting with the egg, followed by spoon and bowl through Sixth, Seventh and Eighth Grades. The simple convex roundness of the egg is the mother of all forms. The spoon also involves convexity on the back of the bowl, concavity in the bowl itself, plus some straightness with the handle. Furthermore, the egg challenges us to create a symmetrical one-part unity, while the spoon challenges us to create a unity from the two different elements of bowl and handle. In Seventh or Eighth Grade the students carve an actual bowl that can be large or small, symmetrical or asymmetrical. The most prominent aspect of a bowl is its hollowed-out concavity. This part should be carved first, for the technical reason that it is easier to secure for carving while the outside shape is still square. But the concavity is carved first and then the outer shape is adapted to the inside concavity in order to emphasize the inward quality that concavity embodies. A bowl must serve a practical function and at the same time it is an artistic experience—one of plumbing the depths of inwardness that resonates with the growing inwardness of the adolescent.

We must concern ourselves with which woodcarving projects to do and when to do them, but I believe the most important issue is *how* we do them. It matters which project we do in relation to the children's developmental stage, but it is only when we consider the different ways we can do these projects that we begin to fathom the reasons why we teach woodcarving in a time when computer skills seem more relevant.

How projects are done is usually left to individual teachers to determine, based on their personal experience and inclination.

This means that many Waldorf woodcarving teachers employ conventional woodworking methods without any awareness for the developmental implications of working in this way relative to other possible ways. Simply stated: conventional woodworking methods employ mostly the sense-nerve side of human nature. Exercising and thereby developing the sense-nerve nature of students is a perfectly valid purpose for teaching woodwork. But it is not the only purpose. Woodwork and particularly woodcarving can offer a way to develop the feeling-will potential of students. At the very least, teachers should have an understanding of and capacity to work in more than one way, so that they can decide which way to work with particular students based on insight rather than personal inclination.

In this context we have reason to consider the qualifications of the teacher. Most schools look for a teacher, a parent or other person in the community who is a woodworker. What should be kept in mind is that most woodworkers today are not woodcarvers. Whether you find a true woodcarver or a woodworker, the chances are that he or she works in a way that is quite professional by conventional standards, but most likely will lack the artistic and pedagogical insight and capacities needed by a Waldorf woodcarving teacher. This is not to say that a Waldorf woodcarving teacher must be a fully trained Waldorf teacher, although such training can only help, wherever possible. On the other hand, it is not essential for a lower school woodcarving teacher to be a professional woodworker.

It is quite possible for a teacher or parent with only limited woodcarving experience to develop the range of skills needed for teaching lower school woodcarving. For a non-professional to master a few basic skills is not so difficult. Sometimes it can be more difficult for a professional woodworker to be satisfied teaching only a small fraction of all he or she has to offer. Concerning technical skill, the professional and non-professional have quite different challenges. But the level of technical skill a teacher brings to teaching woodcarving in the lower school is less important than the artistic and pedagogical insight he must cultivate.

We will explore this artistic/pedagogical dimension of woodcarving by considering the ways we can approach the three classical projects of an egg, a spoon and a bowl. In Chapter 2 we did this to some degree by comparing two different ways to make a spoon. We will continue this method of comparing two ways to do the same project in order to elaborate further the distinction between a thinking-will and a feeling-will approach to woodcarving.

Darning Egg or Top

The symmetrical convexity of an egg form is an ideal first project. However, there is one drawback so fundamental that it forces us to consider alternate projects: the tradition of making an egg as a first project is so well established that it is sometimes forgotten that Steiner's original indication was to make a darning egg. In other words, the egg was not meant to be a purely decorative or sculptural artifact. It was intended to be functional as well as beautiful. Most children today are unaware that there was a time when people did not throw away a sock when it developed a hole. A mere generation or two ago it was commonplace to mend one's socks using an egg-like form inside the sock as an aid to mending the hole. As a form, the egg remains a worthy first project, but it is no longer the perfect project if the functional dimension is not present. Steiner's intent for woodcarving in the lower grades was that the aesthetic and the functional would be united as one.

This has led some woodcarving teachers to seek other projects that would offer a form experience comparable to the egg and at the same time serve a functional purpose. Carving a top seems to meet these dual criteria. A top is clearly functional and has the convex symmetry of the egg. This project also involves carving a small handle to hold and spin the top—darning eggs often had a handle as well. Whether students make tops for their own use or for younger brothers and sisters, most children are clearly motivated by the challenge to make a top that will spin properly. The motivation to achieve symmetry with a darning egg is largely aesthetic, as it would still serve its purpose with less-than-perfect symmetry. With a top, the motivation is directly related to its function. A top is thus a perfect combination of form and function. As the children refine their tops, they will naturally try to spin them. Not only are they keen to spin their own tops; they want to see whose top can spin the longest. If their top wobbles too much and falls down sooner than others', they will want to improve the symmetry. With the egg the teacher often must coax and cajole to get students to improve the symmetry to a reasonable level. With the top the teacher's task is mostly to encourage and guide them in achieving the necessary symmetry.

Although the top can be made freely, this approach makes it difficult to achieve the symmetry. For this reason, a step-by-step, geometric process seems to work best. On the surface, this seems to give the project a thinking-will character, but in fact we shall see that there is plenty of room for exercising the feeling-will. Fig. 21 shows this process in four steps.

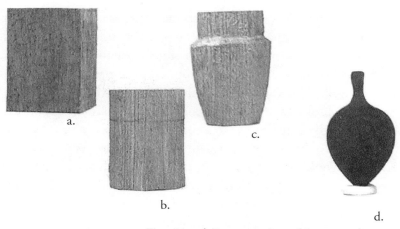

Figs. 21 a-d. Four steps in making a wooden top

1) Tops come in all manner of sizes and proportion, so it is possible to allow some freedom in the size and proportion of the block that is cut. Typically it will be square in breadth and width and somewhat taller to accommodate the spindle. See Figure 21a. Butternut is a wonderful native wood for this purpose, as are basswood and mahogany. Many other woods produce beautiful results but as a first project the wood should not be too hard to work. The critical first step is to draw diagonal lines from corner to corner on the top and bottom surfaces to establish the top and bottom center points. These center points are critical to the final symmetry; marking them with an awl makes it less likely that they will disappear along the way.

2) Some teachers have the children measure off and draw eight vertical lines that will divide the four sides into eight equal sides. It is possible and desirable from the perspec-

tive of exercising feeling-will to refrain from drawing lines and instead have the children rasp down each of the four vertical edges of the block so that

Fig. 21 e.

gradually four new surfaces appear until an eight-sided cylinder is formed. See Fig. 21 e.

3) A line can be drawn around the circumference of this eight-sided cylinder about one-third of the way from the top. With or without such a line, the students continue to rasp the eight surfaces in the top one-third, keeping them vertical and symmetrical as they are reduced towards the top center point. At the same time, the bottom two-thirds is rasped towards the bottom center point but as a gradual curve. See Figure 21 f. Without losing the symmetry of the eight sides continue rasping first the upper and then

Fig. 21 f.

the lower sections towards the center points. At the bottom this process continues until the fine point on which it will spin is created. Gradually, the upper section is formed to create a comfortable handle to hold and spin the top.

4) Only now will the students carefully round off the eight sides with rasp and coarse sandpaper. As long as the symmetry has not gone too far astray, the final step of sanding is very gratifying, as it is not only a matter of smoothing but also of refining the form to get that perfect balance for spinning. Although some of the earlier steps involve the thinking-will, the process necessarily involves feeling more and more as it approaches completion. When it is spun and there is a little wobble, the children must see and feel where it is ever so slightly lop-sided. If there is any drawback to making a top, it is the high degree of symmetry that the children must achieve in order for the top to spin adequately. The experience of the teachers who have made tops with their students suggests that this is not a problem—the teacher must be vigilant in making sure that the two center points are established correctly and are not lost in the process.

Spoons

In Chapter 2 the making of a spoon in two different ways—through a thinking-will and a feeling-will approach—was described in some detail. Here we will review the basic steps of both processes.

A Thinking-Will Spoon

1) When we begin by drawing the outline of a spoon directly onto a block of wood, or on a piece of paper that is then cut out and traced on to the wood, we are proceeding in a thinking-will manner. Once an outline is drawn on the wood, it is only logical to use a saw to cut along the line. For an experienced woodworker in a production situation, a band saw would be the logical choice for cutting out the silhouette of the spoon. Most teachers of lower school are sensitive to the fact that children of this age are not ready to use a band saw. Some teachers decide to cut it out on a band saw themselves for the children. If we want the children themselves to learn to saw, a coping saw is best. See Fig. 22 below.

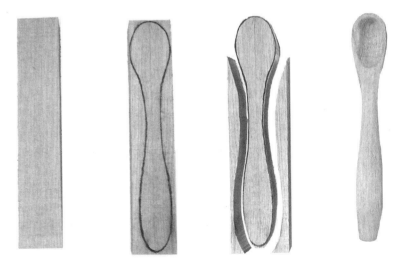

Fig. 22. Thinking-will process of making a wooden spoon

2) Although this conventional approach emphasizes the thinking-will in the first stages, it necessarily becomes more of a feeling-will process in the later stages. The children learn to use a spoon gouge to hollow out the bowl. A rasp is usually the best tool for the back of the bowl, the handle and, most critically, the connecting transition between the bowl and handle.

A Feeling-Will Spoon

1) In this approach it is not necessary to draw anything on the wood. If for some reason we want to help the children visualize a spoon by drawing, then there is a feeling-will way to approach this. Use white chalk, not to draw an outline but to mark the wood as if rounding the corners of the block. In other words, the chalk marks show where one would take away wood if rasping or carving. Slowly we add chalk to indicate where the wood would narrow in the area connecting the bowl and handle. This is a critical step, as it determines the relative size of the bowl and handle. One can continue in this manner, arriving at a final spoon silhouette—the spoon shape will be clear wood surrounded by chalk. It is possible to show how one can go too far, making the connection between the bowl and handle too thin. In this case the purpose of drawing is not to fix the form of the spoon so it can be cut out but to serve as a kind of rehearsal for the carving process. It gives us a feeling for the process of coming to the form gradually as we will when rasping, whittling or carving away the wood. We learn to take away everything that does not look like a spoon. See Fig. 23 below.

Figs. 23 a. Drawing
a spoon in thinking-
will manner.

Figs. 23 b-d. Drawing a spoon in a feeling-will
manner.

2) With or without such a drawing rehearsal, the actual
spoon is begun in the way just described. Using a rasp
we round off the corners and all the edges. Already it
will feel more comfortable in the hand, but will of course
still feel too thick. More must be taken away at the
handle, as well as starting to suggest the shape of the
bowl and the indentation where it connects to the
handle. The children should be encouraged to hold the
wood in their hands regularly to test how it feels—not
just how it looks. Attention should be directed to the
side view as much as the top view (the drawback of the
drawing and cutting approach is that only the top view
is considered and not the side view). See Fig. 24 below.

Fig. 24. Feeling-will process in making a wooden spoon

3) The hollow of the bowl must be carved; it is important to do only a little at a time, starting from the center and only gradually working outward. The final size and shape of the bowl should not be fixed too quickly, but developed in concert with the back of the bowl and the handle. In other words, every part is developed in relation to the whole.

4) The most critical yet subtle aspect of any spoon is the transition between bowl and handle. The size and shape of the bowl should be considered in relation to the expected use of the spoon. The thickness and shape of the handle—how straight and symmetrical or asymmetrical— is a matter of how comfortable and balanced it feels in the hand. The transition between the bowl and handle can become so thin that there is a risk of breaking. Assuming that the grain runs the length of the spoon, this rarely happens. However, even if it is not at risk of actually breaking, it can nevertheless look and feel too thin. Besides the

thinness, there is also the challenge of making the two parts harmonious and not disjointed. Do the two parts of bowl and handle feel physically joined but visually disconnected, or do the two parts form a harmonious whole? See Fig. 25 below.

The processes of rasping and carving serve this need to feel our way to the form gradually. *This is the contemporary reason for teaching woodcarving: to school the feeling-will.* The reasons why the development of the feeling-will is so essential to meeting the challenges of contemporary life are elaborated in Chapter 3.

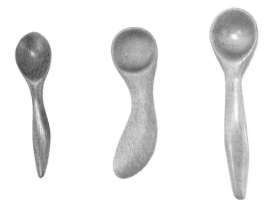

Fig. 25. Variations of spoon design

BOWLS

A Thinking-Will Bowl

1) A bowl can also be approached in a thinking-will manner if we draw the outline of the bowl onto the wood and begin hollowing out the bowl at the line. Even with-

out such a line, some students are so intent on establishing the size and shape they think they want that they start carving at the outer edge. Unfortunately, there is a good chance that novice carvers will not be satisfied with the first shape they create. They will be only more unhappy when they realize that having started at the outer edge their options to change the form are limited.

2) Even if we are more or less content with the inner shape we have created, in this way of working it is natural to excavate most of the wood from the inside as quickly as possible—meaning that we make large tearing and splintering cuts into the wood. This can be smoothed out later so that such roughing out does not affect the final look of the bowl. But besides courting the risk of damage, the main consideration is that this approach does not cultivate a feeling for form. The taking-away process becomes purely quantitative, divorced from qualitative feeling rather than wedding the two together.

3) As with the spoon, a bowl that has been roughed out needs some degree of refining. The student must sooner or later find the necessary feeling for form and the corresponding skill to finish the inside shape. The same applies to carving the outside of the bowl so that the inside and outside are in harmonious relationship to each other. In the end we must exercise our feeling-will to create a beautiful finished bowl. Working in a thinking-will manner enables us to get results more quickly in the early stages but it also postpones and limits what we can do out of our feeling-will in the latter stages.

A Feeling-Will Bowl

1) A bowl can be carved from beginning to end in a feeling-will manner. Again, drawing is not necessary, but if some rehearsal of the process seems in order, then use chalk in the same way as described with the spoon. Rather than drawing the outer edge of the bowl, use chalk to draw a small circular surface in the very center of the block. Slowly enlarge this round surface. After enlarging it a little, try changing the shape from round to oval and then to kidney or other shapes. The point is to experiment, using the chalk surface to explore a number of possibilities as it enlarges to the full size that the block allows. We can do the same coming from the periphery of the block, as if rounding the corners and then gradually finding an outer shape that works well with the inner shape. It may parallel the inner shape, in which case the main thing to determine is how thick or thin to make the lip of the bowl. Or, we can try to find an outer shape that is different from the inside, which means that the thickness of the bowl and lip will vary. When done well, this creates a very dynamic quality; when unsuccessful it will look awkward and clumsy. See Fig. 26 on the next page.

2) Again, with or without drawing, the process of carving proceeds in the same way. Essential to a feeling-will process is the capacity of the student to make clean cuts from first to last. I take considerable time and trouble to demonstrate to the students three factors that make the difference between clean cuts and those that are torn or

splintered. I make clear to them that one of the three is my responsibility, while the other two are up to them. I demonstrate sharpening gouges, but except for buffing I do not expect students to learn to sharpen their tools. Having adequately sharp gouges is the one factor essential to clean cuts that I consider my responsibility to provide. See Appendix.

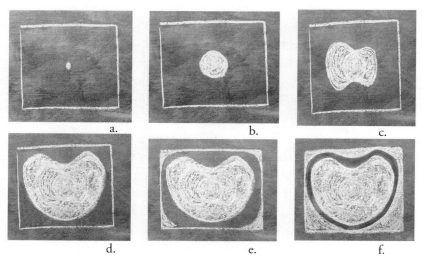

a. b. c.

d. e. f.

Figs. 26 a-f. Drawing a bowl in a feeling-will manner

Even with a sharp tool it is possible to tear and splinter the wood in two different ways. If we carve too deeply, allowing one or both tips of a gouge to go beneath the surface of the wood, some tearing will occur. See Fig. 27.

Fig. 27 a. Making a clean cut

Fig. 27 b. Making a torn or splintered cut

This is not so critical in the early stages, but it is in the finishing. So I expect students to learn to avoid this from the beginning so that it becomes second nature by the time they are in the finishing stage. More serious splintering occurs from carving with, or more accurately, into the grain of the wood. There are different schools of thought about carving with the grain or across the grain. At different times each is useful. The intent to make clean cuts is the only criteria by which to know when to carve with the grain or across it. As long as we have a sharp gouge and do not let the edges go below the surface, we will always produce clean cuts when carving across the grain—especially when the surface we are carving is flat or slightly convex. We get a cleaner, almost polished cut when we carve with the grain, as long as the cut is on a slight downward slope—cutting across the end-grain. When the cut is made with the grain but on a slightly upward slope into the end grain, the gouge will dig in and start to split the wood. See Fig. 28.

Fig. 28 a. Carving with the grain, downward and across the end grain makes a polished cut.

Fig. 28 b. Carving with the grain, upward and into the end grain splinters the wood.

3) I place this much emphasis on the factors that produce clean cuts because in a feeling-will approach, the very first cut in carving a bowl must be a clean cut. In the very center of the block of wood, we carve one small but clean cut with a gouge. See Fig. 29. The edge of such a clean cut will be round or slightly oval and the surface of the cut will be more or less symmetrical. I call this first cut a "seed bowl" because in all respects it looks like a bowl, only a very small one. I call it a "seed bowl" because from this first bowl-like cut, it is possible to make a second and a third cut in such a way that the bowl shape is never lost, but only grows larger and may eventually change its shape. Although we are taking away wood, we can nevertheless feel that the bowl is growing, in the sense that its form evolves organically. See Fig. 30.

Fig. 29. The first clean cut is a "seed bowl."

Fig. 30. The bowl form grows organically from the seed bowl.

4) This organic development of the size and form of the bowl is the key to a process that engages feeling-will. Some people may not produce a clean cut on the first, second or hundredth cut. Trying to make clean cuts is simply the outer aspect of cultivating a different inner process built on the capacity to feel the quality of the form. I will not go into all the other steps and dimensions of carving a bowl. If we get off to a good beginning, exercising our feeling-will from the first cut, everything else will unfold through feeling perception. Fig. 31.

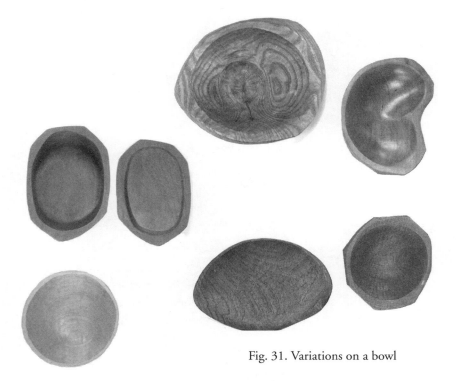

Fig. 31. Variations on a bowl

Movable Toys

This is usually done in the seventh grade, as suggested by Rudolf Steiner, relating to the mechanics main lesson block that comes in this year. I wish here only to draw attention to the possibility of making such a movable toy in a thinking-will manner as compared with a feeling-will approach. Often such toys are made from quarter-inch plywood. With plywood it seems only natural to draw the human or animal form desired onto the surface—with or without drawing it on paper first. It is then cut out with coping saw, sanded, painted and assembled. This kind of process engages the thinking-will of the students. This could be in perfect harmony with the emphasis on mechanics. However, it may also be desirable to use this project in a way that brings together these two sides of our selves—the scientist and the artist. When it comes to the mechanical functioning of the toy, the students must be helped to exercise their thinking-will. But when it comes to forming human and/or animal figures, it is possible to make them in a feeling-will manner. In fact, because the thinking-will predominates even down to the fragmentation of a body into several working parts, it poses an interesting challenge to engage the feeling-will as much as possible. For example, we can try to carve separate limbs made from dimensional stock—perhaps $\frac{3}{4}''$ square or round—rather than plywood. The challenge is to shape the separate parts so that when they are joined together they create a living whole.

HIGH SCHOOL:

In the high school years, the growing physical and mental maturity of our students opens almost limitless possibilities for art and craft activities. There are certain media and projects that seem especially suited to particular grades, but, as we have seen, developmental appropriateness is not the only issue to consider.

In the high school the question of *who* is working with the students is far more important than *what* arts and crafts are offered. In the lower school all subjects, including the arts and crafts, are brought in their all-human dimension rather than as specialist disciplines. In the high school, the opposite is needed; each teacher must stand before the students as a master of his or her field. Thus, in the high school we want artists and craftpersons who are not merely competent but who live and breathe the issues and capacities of their disciplines. We want real scientists, historians and artists. This qualification will have a significant effect on which arts and crafts are brought to the students. Stone carving in Twelfth Grade is wonderful, but does the school have a stonecarver in the community? If the choice lies between an amateur stonecarver and a real wood carver, I would choose the latter in the high school.

There is yet another dimension that must also be consciously worked with in determining who and, only then, which arts and crafts are brought. It is the question of how the artist or craftperson works in his or her medium and therefore how he/she will bring it to the students. In the high school the distinction between the thinking-will and feeling-will approaches to art and craft becomes paramount. In these years our young people should feel more like apprentices to a master than students of a teacher. But what kind of mastery are they to meet? A professional woodworker will teach joinery, a blacksmith the tempering of steel, a painter the creating of realistic landscapes and portraits. But today most professional artists and craftpeople work predominantly in a thinking-will manner. We certainly will want our students to experience such thinking-will ways of working, but we also want them to continue developing their feeling-will. Ideally, a high school will have a balanced mix of artists and craftpeople who have mastered their disciplines in thinking-will and feeling-will directions.

It may be helpful to note that the words, *art* and *craft*, can mean different things. They can refer not merely to different mediums, but to differences in purpose. Art usually means the fine arts of painting and sculpture that serve a soul/spiritual function rather than a particular physical function. The crafts, by contrast, are usually meant to serve a practical function as well as have an aesthetic appeal. The distinction between art and craft is not really a matter of medium, because both artist and craftperson can use the same material. A potter uses clay for the craft of making pots, while a sculptor may use the same clay to model a head. A woodworker may make furniture with the same wood that a woodcarver uses to carve a human or abstract form. If we use art to signify aesthetic value and craft to mean functional value, then we must say that there is art in every craft and craft in every art.

There is another way to understand these terms. Craft can describe a head and hand or thinking-will activity, whereas art can mean a head, heart and hand or feeling-will activity. In this sense an artist who works in a thinking-will manner emphasizes the *craft of his/her art*, while a craftperson who works in a feeling-will manner emphasizes the *art of his/her craft.*

Such considerations may sound abstract on paper, but they are quite significant in determining the developmental experience we want for high school students. We want a good spectrum of art and craft activities guided by master artists and craftpeople. And in addition we have every reason to try to provide, not simply a balanced mix of arts and crafts, but a mix of thinking-will arts and crafts and feeling-will arts and crafts.

With these perspectives as our foundation, we will consider just a few examples to indicate how this might manifest in the high school.

NINTH AND TENTH GRADES
Platonic Solids
The Platonic solids have an important place in Seventh or Eighth Grade and again in Ninth Grade. Often these geometric forms are drawn on paper, cut out and assembled. This is an excellent thinking-will exercise. In addition, the Platonic solids can be made in a feeling-will manner by modeling them in clay. A tetrahe-

dron modeled in clay may lack the precision of a constructed one, but the inner and outer activity of adjusting the clay on all sides to achieve the required symmetry is invaluable. The juxtaposition between the geometry of the forms modeled in an organic process allows the students to develop objective clarity in a way that is

Fig. 32. The organic transformation of a ball into a tetrahedron

not mechanistic but intuitive. See Fig. 32. Furthermore, whereas the constructed solids are made as separate forms, in clay they are transformed from one form into another in a lawful and ordered manner. For a fuller description of how to make all five solids in clay so that they transform one into the other in a particular order, see *Learning About the World Through Modeling* by Arthur Auer.

In addition to doing these transformations in clay, it is possible for Ninth Grade students to make one or more Platonic solids in wood. In order to emphasize the contrast between a thinking-will and a feeling-will approach, we can make a tetrahedron, for example, in two different ways. For the thinking-will, draw the four triangular sides onto $1/4''$ or $1/8''$ plywood and cut them out with a coping saw. The edges must be beveled carefully in order to glue the sides together. See Figure 33. For the feeling-will, the students can carve the same tetrahedron from a block of wood approximately the same size as the constructed one. See Fig. 34. In the end the two tetrahedrons will look almost identical. The similarity in the final forms will only heighten the contrast between the two ways in which they were made. Whether students appreciate it consciously or not at the time, the making of two tetrahedrons in two different ways

Fig. 33. A tetrahedron
constructed from plywood

Fig. 34. A tetrahedron
carved from hard wood

will resonate in them in the years ahead as a concrete experience of the difference between their thinking-will and feeling-will.

If we can work in such contrasting ways with the Platonic solids, we can do the same with almost any project. Construct a box with simple or more exotic joints and then carve a box with a lid. Construct a picture frame and then carve a frame. Construct a stool or table and then carve a stool or table. Of course, we can design a project to be mostly thinking-will with a little feeling-will or vice versa. Or we can do a thinking-will project one term or one year and a feeling-will project another. Broadly speaking, the objectivity of the thinking-will is especially appropriate in Ninth and Tenth Grade.

Another project that seems especially suited to Ninth and Tenth Grades is modeling a head that begins young and is then transformed into an older face. This can be done as a mask, but doing it in the round and life-size or larger works especially well for this age (especially for the boys). Begin by coiling a one-foot high

Fig. 35

"light bulb" or "chess pawn" shape with fairly thick walls, at least one inch. See Fig. 35. From this we develop the overall spherical shape partially through pushing but also by adding clay. We subdivide the overall spherical form with a slight indentation across the middle of the front half of the form where the eyes will come later. See Fig. 36. We then subdivide the lower lobe of the front with two more slight indentations that give us the two cheeks and the area of the mouth. This subdivision into larger and smaller lobes, plus a little nub for a nose and two small swellings for the eyes, gives us the main elements of a child's head. See Fig. 37. Although we have indicated the eyes and nose, it is important that the students hold back for several sessions from developing the eyes, mouth and ears. The reason for this is that they must get these bumps and hollows to look like a human child and not an alien or some other aberration of the human form. The humanness must depend not on the details of eyes, mouth and hair, but on the harmonious configuration and proportions of the bumps and hollows.

After developing the child's head, I demonstrate on my example how to transform a head from young to old. This is mostly a matter of pressing in the cheeks, nose and chin to become more flat and pointed, and hollowed. See Fig. 38. This transformation from young to old is particularly captivating for high school students at this age. This polar experience of budding and withering life is the primary pedagogical reason for doing this project in this way and at this time. Working with budding and withering is the sculptural equivalent of black-and-white drawing.

Fig. 36 a.

Fig. 36 b.

Fig. 37 a.

Fig. 37 b.

Fig. 38 a.

Fig. 38 b.

Sometimes I require the students to transform their "children" into older faces. For some, especially girls, this can be a traumatic experience. As a compromise I allow those who want to keep their child head to complete it and then make a second head. They start the same way as described above, but once the main convex lobes are in place, they transform this form into the older head. Another approach I have tried recently is to give them the option of making either a more youthful face or an older one. However, I ask that the young face must not only be beautiful but it must also have character. Conversely, an older head must not only have strong character but it must also have beauty. The emphasis can be more on beauty or on character but both must be evident. In this way we avoid heads that are blatantly ugly in the grotesque sense as well as heads that have a sentimental or over-ripe kind of beauty.

ELEVENTH AND TWELFTH GRADES

Again, much depends on who is available to work in the upper grades. Where there is a master woodworker, I have seen Eleventh and Twelfth Graders build incredible furniture, musical instruments, canoes and kayaks. There is no question that some students in Eleventh and Twelfth Grades can be guided to develop high levels of technical skill. It is equally true that these students are mature enough to appreciate and explore contemporary approaches to art. My experience is primarily with wood and stone carving.

Where I can work with the same students first in Eleventh Grade and then again in Twelfth, I have them carve wood in Eleventh and stone in Twelfth. If for some reason I have them only in Grade Twelve, I let them choose wood or stone. With woodcarving

124

they can carve a relief or a sculpture in the round. The stone carving is done with a moderate-sized block of marble or limestone. Whatever the material or size, my one requirement is that the block of wood or stone becomes a form that expresses life and movement. In the first instance I actively discourage them from having a preconceived idea of what it will become, for instance a human or animal form. Everything is focused on their discovering how to create living movement through attending to where and how they take away material. If they take away from the top, the form will feel heavier or more grounded. If they take away near the bottom, the form will seem to lift upwards. As they take away from top or bottom, they will create indentations that flow into bulging lobes. I ask the students to create free forms that emphasizes this feeling of flowing undulation that arises from larger and smaller convex lobes and double-bent hollows. See Fig. 39.

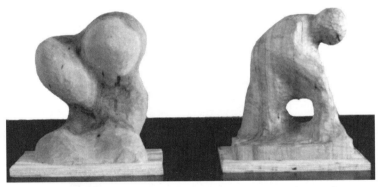

Fig. 39. Freeform and human form—both carved out of gesture

This free form process can take the better half of a course. Some students are more disposed than others to working with pure qualities of form without reference to human or animal forms, but it would be a lost opportunity if we did not engage juniors and seniors with these contemporary issues and approaches to art. As their stone and wood carving progresses, the students are free to continue developing their sculpture as free forms, or if they are so inclined, they can bring out any human or animal form that they see emerging. With a representational figure there is still the challenge of how to draw out the details in an organic and intuitive process rather than just sticking them in. In that sense it continues to call upon their feeling-will.

A wonderful culmination for the visual arts is to work on a large mural or sculpture project as a group. For example, carving a large sign provides an excellent practical application of carving that can be worked on by three or four students at a time. If there is no need for a sign, then a large sculptural relief for a school wall or a free standing stone sculpture could be a gift to the whole school, as well as providing a lesson in social sculpture. Large reliefs in clay or seed drawings as described in kindergarten and lower school can be re-visited as a warm-up to such group projects in wood or stone. See Fig. 40 and Fig. 41.

Fig. 40 a.

Fig. 40 b.

Fig. 40 c.

Fig. 40 d.

Figs. 40 a-g. Group sculptures

Fig. 40 e.

Fig. 40 f.

Fig. 40 g.

Fig. 41 a.

Fig. 41 b.

Figs. 41 a and b. Group drawing

As students are about to step out into the real world, such group artistic exercises and projects give them a glimpse of the social relevance of the artistic faculties they have been developing over the years. By the final year the students are mature enough and often hungry to understand consciously the deeper significance of all the artistic activity they have been exposed to. It will be a great source of strength and health for these students to finish high school with some conscious awareness of the reason the arts were such a fundamental part of their schooling. At the core of their being they will be profoundly grateful to know that the arts and crafts played a vital role in developing their full human potential, the artist as much as the scientist in them, their feeling-will as much as their thinking-will.

Sharpening Carving Tools

This section on sharpening is for both experienced and less experienced woodcarving teachers. If you are teaching woodcarving with a minimum of practical expertise, it is essential that you learn to sharpen gouges well and efficiently. Unless you can provide sharp tools, it is actually better not to have a woodcarving program—dull tools undermine any other value woodcarving may have for students. Unless you can sharpen fairly quickly, you will be overwhelmed by the amount of re-sharpening that is typically required. The following is offered in part as a starting point for those who have not yet mastered the craft of sharpening. For the experienced woodcarver, for whom sharpening is second nature and simply a practical necessity, I offer a fuller perspective that includes the developmental significance of mastering both the art and science of sharpening gouges. In teaching woodcarving, we must be able to sharpen tools well. In an educational context it is relevant to see it also as a way to exercise and thereby develop both thinking-will and feeling-will.

The science of sharpening enables us to have a clear understanding of what we must do in order to make our gouges truly sharp. Sharpening is a science insofar as there is no place for wishful thinking, good luck or divine intervention. There are jigs and other mechanical devices that can save us the time and trouble of developing the understanding and skill to sharpen gouges ourselves. In that case we get the results without developing any capacity. If we are to produce sharp tools, we must know what we are doing and must also be able to co-ordinate head and hand towards very precise results. The practical skill of sharpening may seem like an applied science, but this is only one part. We shall see that it is also an art that calls for head, heart and hand co-ordination or feeling-will.

The Science of Sharpening

Most people assume that a sharp gouge is simply a tapered, knife-like edge. However, when we first try sharpening we may feel frustrated and disheartened at how dull our tool remains after we have spent considerable time and effort creating a razor-thin edge. What is the elusive difference between two edges that to the naked eye look equally thin, but where one cuts like butter while the other does nothing more than rip and tear the wood? There is more to sharpening a gouge than meets the eye, but that is not to say we need a microscope. We need to develop a finer eye, guided by insight.

First we must come to see that sharpness is not black or white but a spectrum from useless, to dull, to sharp, to sharpest. Often a gouge will make a clean cut but not like butter. Such a gouge may have cut like butter earlier, but with use and buffing it no longer cuts as well as it once did. With some practice, we can learn to look at the bevel of a gouge to see subtle differences in its shape.

By definition a gouge is a curved edge—it is a chisel when the edge is straight. If the edge is curved, the surface of the bevel will also be curved across the width of the tool. But a bevel will also have one of three possible shapes in its shorter, lengthwise direction (typically, the width of the bevel of a gouge is greater than its length). This is best seen from the side of the tool where the edge and bevel form a kind of "V." At a glance we may assume the bevel is straight, but it may be a convex curve or a concave curve. A gouge that does not cut very well often has a convex bevel. Compared to a gouge with a straight or concave bevel, one that is convex creates more resistance as the edge enters the wood. A straight bevel will draw well, and one that is concave even better, as the volume of the bevel diminishes. We shall see that there is no one right kind of bevel because there are situations where each of the three possibilities may be desirable. See Fig. 42.

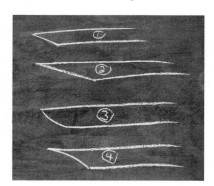

Fig. 42. #1 is a short bevel; #2 is a long bevel; #3 is a convex bevel; and #4 is a concave bevel.

Another variable to be aware of is the difference between a short and a long bevel. A bevel that tapers for a greater distance is thinner and therefore will slice into the wood more readily than a short, thicker bevel. An experienced woodcarver does not always keep the bevel on his gouges the same length or shape. When roughing out on fairly hard wood, a long, thin and/or concave bevel is prone to break. In this case a shorter and possibly convex bevel may do the best job. When doing careful finishing on softer wood, a short convex bevel will not be as

133

helpful as a long straight or concave bevel. We will return to the practical way to achieve these different bevels when we turn to the art of sharpening. For now, it belongs to the science of sharpening to understand that there are different sizes and shapes that can be given to the bevel of a gouge and that we may choose one or the other according to the type of carving we are doing.

The most critical aspect of the science of sharpening is knowing when a gouge is truly sharp without guessing or even testing it on a piece of wood. Every woodcarver will have his or her favorite sharpening stone and technique. The diversity of approaches can be quite bewildering and confusing to someone learning to sharpen. With all the different tools and techniques to choose from, in the end there is only one thing that matters: you must be able to produce a *burr* along the length of the edge.

Whether sharpening by hand on a stone or on a grinding wheel, the critical goal is to wear down the metal until it is so thin that it curls. That curled metal is a burr. Only when that burr is created and then carefully worn away is the edge as sharp as possible. Sharpening by hand is slower; it requires more patience and perseverance to wear down the metal until the burr is visible. Grinding on a wheel is obviously faster, but without the proper care or an appropriate grinding wheel (do not use a regular carborundum wheel, but a softer one designed for the finer metal of carving tools), the metal can "lose its temper." This occurs when the metal gets too hot and turns black. The metal is no longer hard enough to keep a sharp edge and will become dull right away. Dip the edge of the tool in water occasionally to keep it cool.

The Art of Sharpening

We are now ready to translate our theoretical understanding of sharpening into practice. I will describe the process on an electric grinder, as this is the more common but more difficult skill to master. We will assume that we have a tool that no longer responds to buffing but has a convex bevel or has a nick in the edge that produces a white line when we carve. This white line is actually the nick tearing instead of cutting the wood. In this case, we hold the gouge square to the wheel so as to grind the whole edge down until the nick is gone. This will make the edge thicker and thus impossible to cut into the wood.

Most electric grinders rotate towards us and therefore strike the tool in a downward direction. For this reason we will see sparks streaming downward from the tool as it touches the wheel. The sparks are tiny bits of metal burning up that quickly become gray dust—they do not hurt when they hit our hand. The first and most crucial thing to determine is the angle at which we hold the gouge to the wheel. If we hold it more horizontally, it will create a short bevel, more vertically and it will become a longer bevel. As we discussed above there is no right or wrong length of bevel although a medium length serves most purposes. If we are new to sharpening, it is natural to be intimidated by the speed and noise of the machine, and so it may take a few tries and checking the bevel before we find the angle for the bevel we want. It is challenging enough to find the right angle; it is even more difficult to maintain the same angle until we have produced a burr. It only takes the slightest movement up or down to produce two or more bevels instead of one. Learning to hold the angle of our bevel is mostly a matter of practice. If we do not want to destroy our expensive gouges, we can use a 3/4″ wide stripe of metal from a hardware store and practice to our hearts' content.

Maintaining a constant angle is both a science and an art. I help myself by holding my arm against my side and locking my wrist to minimize any tendency to move up and down. However, it is also a matter of feel. With repetition we can begin to feel whether the tool is staying at the same angle or has shifted a little. Watching the stream of sparks is also a crucial aid; we can look for the mo-

ment when sparks begin to bounce off the tip. This tells us that the edge is getting so thin that a burr is about to form. However, it is only when a small stream of sparks begins to flow over the top and, as we rotate the tool, along the full length of the edge, that we know we have the all-important burr. See Fig 43.

Fig. 43.

We must wear off this burr by continuing the process on a fine stone—an Indian combination stone for example. We place the bevel on the stone, making sure it is neither too high nor too low, in order to establish the same angle of the bevel. We can determine if we are getting the right angle by checking the bevel after a few strokes. If the gouge is held too vertically, we will see that only the tip is being worn down; if too horizontally only the heel of the bevel will show wear. Only when both the tip and heel are wearing down will we know that we have the right angle. We can also note that a slight hollow is visible in the middle area of the bevel. This shows us that in fact the whole bevel has become concave from the convex curve of the grinding wheel. See Fig. 43. We lose some of this concavity in taking away the burr, but it is not necessary to take away all the concavity by making the bevel flat. A little concavity is often desirable. Furthermore, if we make it flat, it will only become convex sooner from subsequent buffing. After working on the bevel side, we use a hard Arkansas stone to wear down the bevel from the topside of the edge. It is important to move the stone back and forth, flush to the top surface of the gouge. We work back and forth on the bevel side and then on the topside until eventually the burr separates from the edge and falls off. After a few passes on a buffing wheel with compound, we have a perfectly sharp gouge that will truly cut like butter.

I knew a woodcarving teacher who required his adult students to learn to sharpen their tools before beginning to carve. As an abstract principle there is merit in saying that a student must learn to sharpen a gouge before carving with one. In practice, however, this makes little sense for the simple reason that most people would never get to the actual carving. Learning to sharpen gouges well and efficiently takes years of practice. Therefore, I do not expect, nor do I in fact want, lower school, high school or adult students trying to sharpen tools. By the same token, it is not acceptable for students to take sharp gouges for granted; it is essential that they have an appreciation and respect for the time and skill that is needed to provide them with sharp gouges. For this reason, I dedicate part of one lesson, a few sessions into a course, for a thorough introduction and demonstration of both the science and art of sharpening gouges as described in the foregoing. If one or two students have a special interest and aptitude, I will let them learn on a scrap of metal. Otherwise, all students learn to buff their tools.

Although most students do not learn to sharpen gouges, I use my introduction to the science of sharpening and my demonstration of the art of sharpening as yet another opportunity to raise into consciousness the thinking-will and feeling-will dimensions of our humanity. It is a way I can tangibly demonstrate to my students that as their teacher I strive to develop both the scientist and the artist in myself, both my thinking-will and feeling-will.

BIBLIOGRAPHY

Alexandra, John. *Mephistopheles' Anvil*, Spring Valley, NY: Rose Harmony Publications, 1996.

Archiati, Pietro. *From Christianity to Christ*, London, England: Temple Lodge Publishing, 1996.

Auer, Arthur. *Learning about the World through Modeling*, Fair Oaks, CA: AWSNA Publications, 2001.

Barfield, Owen. *Saving the Appearances,* Hanover, NH: Wesleyan University Press, 1988.

Bortoft, Henri. *The Wholeness of Nature*, Hudson, NY: Lindisfarne Press, 1996.

Brull, Dieter. *The Mysteries of Social Encounter*, Fair Oaks, CA: AWSNA Publications, 2002.

Clausen, Anke, and Martin Riedel. *Plastisches Gestalten (Sculptural Forming),* Stuttgart: Mellinger Verlag, 1985.

—————————. *Plastisches Gestalten mit Holz (Sculptural Forming in Wood)*, Stuttgart: Mellinger Verlag, 1985.

Martin, Michael, editor. *Educating through Arts and Crafts*, Forest Row, England: Steiner Schools Fellowship Publications, 1999.

Mitchell, David, and Patricia Livingston. *Will-Developed Intelligence*, Fair Oaks, CA: AWSNA Publications, 1999.

Niederhauser, Hans, and Margret Frohlich. *Form Drawing*, New York: Mercury Press, 1974.

Read, Herbert. *Education through Art*, New York: Pantheon Books (Random House), 1956.

—————————. *The Education of Free Men*, London, England: Freedom Press, 1944.

Richards, M.C. *Toward Wholeness*, Middletown, CT: Wesleyan University Press, 1980.

Schiller, Friedrich. *On the Aesthetic Education of Man*, New York: Frederick Ungar Publishing, 1981.

Steiner, Rudolf, and Michael Howard. *Art as Spiritual Activity*, Hudson, NY: Anthroposophic Press, 1998.

Steiner, Rudolf. *Art in the Light of Mystery Wisdom*, London, England: Rudolf Steiner Press, 1970.

—————————. *The Arts and Their Mission*, New York: Anthroposophic Press, 1964.

—————————————. *Balance in Teaching*, Spring Valley, NY: Mercury Press, 1990.

—————————————. *Discussions with Teachers*, Hudson, NY: Anthroposophic Press, 1997.

—————————————. *Education as a Social Problem*, Spring Valley, NY: Anthroposophic Press, 1984.

—————————————. *The Fall of the Spirits of Darkness*, London, England: Rudolf Steiner Press, 1995.

—————————————. *The Foundations of Human Experience,* New York: Anthroposophic Press, 1996.

—————————————. *Human Values in Education*, London, England: Rudolf Steiner Press, 1971.

—————————————. *Intuitive Thinking as a Spiritual Path*, Hudson, NY: Anthroposophic Press, 1995.

—————————————. *Practical Advice to Teachers*, Great Barrington, MA: Anthroposophic Press, 2000.

—————————————. *Preparing for the Sixth Epoch*, Spring Valley, NY: Anthroposophic Press, 1979.

—————————————. *The Social Future*, Spring Valley, NY: Anthroposophic Press, 1972.

—————————————. *Theosophy*, New York: Anthroposophic Press, 1971.

————————. *The Younger Generation,* New York: Anthroposophic Press, 1967.